A. A. AIEBRAHEEM

5 ESSENTIAL DIMENSIONS:

HOW TO BALANCE YOUR LIFE FOR HEALTH, SUCCESS AND CONTENTMENT

Dedication:

To my parents, who sowed my seed

And watered my buds

And fed my leaves

And protected my roots

Till I became a tree among the living

My book is the fruit

Acknowledgement, courtesy and dedication to them.

I also dedicate this book to every person searching for

knowledge.

INTRODUCTION

What Are The 5 Essential Dimensions?

Our lives are made up of five elements that are constantly changing; our financial, social, internal, physical and spiritual affairs. To live a healthy, successful and tranquil existence, we need to bring each of these life dimensions into equilibrium. Striving to achieve equilibrium in these five key dimensions will increase our humanity, advance our progress, bring us greater financial rewards, instill a greater love for other people, and a better understanding of ourselves, our bodies and our souls.

The purpose of this book is to show why we cannot reach our potential as individuals unless all five of these life dimensions are balanced. If we neglect any one of them, the ensuing disharmony destroys our tranquility and can wreck our lives.

The 5 Essential Dimensions is an attempt to prevent this happening. It is a comforting counterweight to the lure of money, a steadying influence on the bodies that carry us, a stable platform for the social ladders that we rise up on, and a net that protects us from falling. It is a compass for our thoughts, and a safeguard for the soul that will remain after our bodies have perished. When the prescription in *The 5 Essential Dimensions* is followed it will bring us tranquility and satisfaction, making us better prepared to enjoy life's happy moments and to cope with its sad ones.

Think of the five equilibriums we are reaching for as buildings. Each day we add to them a little, and with repeated efforts day-by-day we raise them slowly to their full height. Four of the five are places for us to inhabit during our lives. Building them will bring us satisfaction, and we shall enjoy the time we spend in them. They will bring us sufficient money to meet our needs, many worthwhile friends, and a sense of spiritual well-being and inner calm that make us envied. These four will lay the spiritual foundations for our passage to the fifth, the one we will enjoy in the hereafter, and which will shelter our soul for eternity.

Why this book matters

Today, we are witnessing enormous advances in the fields of science and commerce. The invention of products that make our lives simpler, shorten distances, and provide comfort and luxury. These products are the result of better design, endless creativity, advanced manufacturing techniques and slick marketing.

Whereas once we had to search for solutions to our problems, today we are overwhelmed by products that do everything for us, and we are pursued through each day by clever advertisements that come to haunt our thoughts. We have become obsessed with perfection and quality. No sane person could resist the charm and temptation of a luxurious car, the thrill of traveling on a gigantic aircraft, or the allure of owning the latest smartphone. It is all an unparalleled achievement. But it is an achievement of the world of commerce, in the pursuit of profit, and one that it is driven solely by the desire for money. Its sole guiding principle is that if it is profitable, it is good.

Astonishing new discoveries and inventions no longer astonish us. In fact we barely notice them, so accustomed are we to seeing them arrive, become obsolete, and disappear like firework trails into the sky.

Unfortunately some of us are mere bystanders, standing apart from this great achievement, like people not yet touched by the civilization that has gripped the rest of our world. These unfortunates watch science and its accomplishments without deriving any benefit from it. Picture such a man. He lives in a cave, or in the middle of a forest. Perhaps he is a subsistence farmer, standing outside the walls of his village near a remote airstrip, watching a plane landing that seems to be heading straight for his village. After it has passed and dazzled him he picks up his spear and returns to his farm, neither wondering how it flies, nor where it comes from, or where it goes.

There is no shame in refusing to keep up with technology, or in failing to acquire the latest devices. It is a personal choice. The shame is in failing to be human. Science has the potential to benefit us greatly as people, but these benefits are only harvested if they serve the pursuit of profit, for they are harvested by people who live only for money. Living at the heart of our civilization they chase money like a lion runs after its prey. They take no care for friends, nor for family, nor for their neighbors. A lion at least returns to look after its cubs after devouring its prey, but these people are delinquent with their children for lack of time. They neglect their parents, and do not ask after their families, because it would be an unnecessary distraction to the pursuit of making money. Money is all that counts. They socialize for the purpose of making money, they eat, drink and sleep for the purpose of making money. Money is the focus of their lives.

They are prisoners of an illusion. The only beauty they can see is in figures. They abandon their principles and avoid the inconvenient restraint of ethics. Such distractions would hinder their scrabbling for money, which becomes the main focus of their lives. They gorge on food without asking whether they are being greedy, and consume friendship like a commodity, without asking themselves whether their friends are genuine. Then, on a day they had failed to prepare for, they are struck by incurable diseases, or find that their close friends have become implacable enemies. When their lives are finally exhausted they die, leaving behind all the money that had been the focus of their existence because such thoughts did not help them make money.

My utmost sorrow for these people are the reason I am writing this book. It saddens me that some people do not understand that life is a test; and that all its questions end with answers chosen by ourselves. But these people do not choose in the real sense of the word. Throughout their lives they follow a blind path, stumbling into answers without thinking: they work in the first profession that comes their way, without searching for a more fitting one; they befriend whoever smiles at them, rather than look for a faithful friend. This is how they live their lives. Where, then, is the choice? And what is their score in the test when their life comes to an end?

We live with many creatures on this planet. We share air and food and water with them, and we are superior to them not because we are stronger or because we are taller, but only because we know how to choose and they do not. If we squander the precious gift of choice, we forfeit our superiority. We return to being no better than animals.

This book is for those unfortunate people who fail to choose, but it also for you and me, to help us rise to a higher plane and see the world as it really is. It proposes that we take control of our lives, trim our sails to suit our own personal goals, and learn how to make a conscious choice about the direction in which to steer. Otherwise we drift aimlessly, letting the winds of fate drive us where we do not want to go. Unless we make choices we will be buffeted by waves, and sooner or later capsized. It is the conscious act of planning and choosing that keeps our lives on track. And that makes us human.

Chapter 1: insight for living

Misery

I sit on a chair, discretely watching passersby and trying to judge their characters from their appearance and behavior.

A man in his mid-forties appears, with long hair falling so low over his eyes his vision is obscured. I watch from a distance as he raises his hands and flicks back his hair like a girl. The action is unconscious, a habitual gesture as he stands in the queue waiting to pay for his coffee. Looking at his watch he lifts his head, casts a furtive glance at something on his neighbor's clothing, runs his fingers through his hair then flicks it back again, before tilting his head to let it fall once more across his face. From the way he repeats these actions it is plain that he admires its length and enjoys feeling its softness against his fingers.

When the scene repeats itself I begin spinning scenarios in my head, casting the man as the imaginary hero in each. Then he pays for his coffee and rushes out. I try to understand why he wanted such long hair; for it was graying, his youth was long past, and baldness was advancing across his scalp. Why would a man of his age feel the need to wear his hair so long, when it was obviously not suited to him? Since I could never know his reasons I let my imagination loose to devise an explanation.

Perhaps he was handsome when he was young, with long, well-styled hair. And perhaps after styling it a pretty young woman, who had previously ignored him, once came and cast a shy glance in his direction.

Fascinated by his hair she could not look away, even when he stared straight into her eyes.

Confused and embarrassed she finally pulled her gaze aside, only to have it pulled back to him. The glances led to a smile, the smile become mutual, and a conversation struck up. As she was a regular at the coffee shop they became well acquainted. When at last he asked what she saw in him, she told him that she likes his hair. Her story ended there, but the story of his hair continued. He cherishes the memory and won't let it fade, repeating it endlessly in his imagination, even though the handsomeness of his youth is long gone.

This story is a brief illustration of the sadness inherent in the human condition. To find this sadness we do not need a guidebook. It is all around us. Just look and you will see a wealthy man whose body is in constant pain despite his wealth, a woman whose clothes show she is trying hopelessly to recapture her youth, a man who neglects his family, and a whole stream of men and women who cannot accept the reality of their lives. Imprisoned within an empty existence they take refuge in a fantasy world, finding one excuse after another to avoid returning to confront the reality of their lives. They cut themselves off, and even if you speak to them about their condition they cannot hear you. They have lost the ability to engage with the world, lost interest in what is happening around them, and even lost the will to care.

If these observations seem to deviate from the topic of my book, understand that my motive is to describe a condition that touches us all. The human condition is filled with misery. It is the same among all peoples, and all lands. I know this from my own personal misery, but also from observing the sadness of people I know, and of people I observe, and of the people I spend time with. We are all touched by misery. The wise among us are intimately familiar with the causes of our misery, the less wise are less aware of it; but it touches us all.

Happiness

Although we each have a different idea of what happiness is, we nevertheless recognize it when we experience it. Our personal concept of happiness dictates our actions and controls our minds. People who like fishing think about fishing even when they cannot actually get out to fish. They avidly follow fishing-related news, study the weather and wind charts, and talk about fishing-related topics, because fishing memories are ingrained into their thoughts.

Those people whose happiness lies in gathering money, we find them always busy looking for profitable opportunities, and monitoring markets and indices. While those who find happiness in a bottle believe it is to be found in their favorite vintage. They plan when and where they will buy it, look forward to drinking it, and never tire of talking about its fine flavor.

Every one of us seeks happiness in our own way. Some watch sport, or date girls. While others collect rare items. Whatever our belief, ideology or taste, we all believe that we can find happiness if we search hard enough, and we pursue it like a cure. But does this happiness really exist?

Where is happiness found?

What really makes people happy? Imagine asking a man to list all the things he would need for happiness, and then giving him all he dreams of. On top we will add anything he seems to have left out. Our fortunate man will be given a grand house to live in, perfect health, and the means to enjoy himself. After two years we would go back and ask him how he feels, only to find that the things he asked for, and the extra gifts we gave him, are no longer of interest.

That is how we all are: what makes us happy as children will not make us happy as adults, and what makes us happy today will not make us happy tomorrow. So what is the happiness that we continue to chase without knowing its true nature? And where do we find it?

Three researchers[1] from two American universities – the University of North West and the University of Massachusetts – prepared a study on the happiness of twenty-two lottery winners, compared to controls. At the end of the study it showed that the lottery winners were no happier than

---

1 *Lottery Winners and Accident Victims: Is Happiness Relative* Philip Brickman & Dan Coates, 1978. Journal of Personality and Social Psychology, 36, 917-927.

the controls. The study demonstrated that happiness is relative to our situation. It has no connection with the amount of money or property we own, or even our good health.

Happiness is accidental

If you are seeking happiness, here is news that will not make you happy. Everlasting joy does not exist on earth; anyone searching for it will be disappointed, and anyone who claims it is either bragging or trying to sell something. There are many peddlers of a false illusion of happiness; this is the role of cinemas, films, clubs and other purveyors of artificial joy. But are these things the same as genuine joy? Or simply marketing tools, selling happiness as a commodity like bread or insurance?

How can we be happy when we are not immune to sickness? How can we enjoy life when we are not immune to pain? The only true happiness is everlasting happiness; transient joy that is replaced by misery is not happiness in any real sense. It is not the kind of happiness we dream of.

The question has to be – is happiness really possible? I doubt that anyone has ever attained lasting happiness in the past. But we can perhaps attain contentment; a state that is less elevated than happiness, but more enduring.

Although life offers many pleasures, the people who purvey these pleasures conveniently forget to warn us that they are temporary pleasures. The sweetness of food fades in moments, and even the tastiest dishes fail to impress us for long. Their pleasure may be intense for a few moments, but it is ephemeral; by the time the food has been swallowed, the pleasure has ended.

Yet somehow in our minds we transform these fleeting moments into something more enduring. Remembering a delicious meal, we transform it in our memory into a long, meandering course of endless pleasure. When in fact, the pleasure was just a series of short-lived moments.

All life's vanities are short-lived. But a combination of desire and imagination change them into something more enduring in our memory. It is these false memories that trick us into believing that we should strive for enduring happiness, when we ought to know that such happiness does not exist.

Why the absence of everlasting happiness is important

We seem to have forgotten that as human beings we are travelers who will one day leave this world. During our time on earth we progress from stages of growth and development towards an inevitable exit. Travelers cannot afford the luxury of tarrying if they want to move forward. Sad as it may be, the absence of permanent happiness keeps our vision clear and our logic sharp. It acts as an essential spur that drives us to be inventive and resourceful. If permanent happiness could be attained, we would lose the will to advance, to strive for improvements in science and technology, to overcome the obstacles that life throws in our path. It is longing, striving, and seeking solutions to the problems that make our lives hard, that have brought our great scientific advances. Without these challenges, would science have achieved even 1% of what we can do today?

The limitation on the pleasure available during our lives exists for a reason. We will examine this reason later, in the chapter on Spiritual Equilibrium.

Why search for happiness?

Both the Old Testament and the Quran tell a similar story of Adam, the first man, who threw happiness away, and was consigned by God to live a harsh life scratching a living from the earth. Earth is not a place where everlasting and permanent happiness is found. Looking for it here is a distraction that diverts us from pursuing moderate contentment and peace of mind. These are the goals we should be pursuing, as they are more easily within our reach.

Yet even knowing this, our desire for an impossible goal still drives us. In our dreams we see our parents as far happier than they really were, and we want to achieve the same. The pull of that dream is so strong we cannot easily let it go, even though it corrupts our thoughts, leads us astray, and plants the seed of destructive desires.

Sexual desire, for example, does not bring permanent happiness. To the contrary, we become animals, obsessed with chasing sexual pleasure for its own end. There are many pleasures other than sex that await human beings, and they are actually more likely to make our lives fulfilling. Researchers [2]from the University of Carnegie recently published a study which considered the question: "Does having a lot of sex improve our sense of happiness?" The study concluded that there is no correlation between having a lot of sex and feeling happy. The result is not surprising, as there has never been any evidence that indulging in excessive sex improves a person's mood. And pursuing any one physical pleasure to excess dulls our appetite for spiritual and intellectual pleasures, and inhibits us from enjoying them. We may even forget that they exist, so focused do we become on bodily lust. Yet in the long run these other pursuits are likely to bring greater satisfaction.

In reality we are poor judges of how to maximize our enjoyment. We invest our time and energy in activities that bring only limited rewards. We may believe that having children will bring us happiness. But how often does it do so? We may think that owning a fine house will bring us happiness. But once we move in, how long will it be before the attraction fades? We may believe that amassing a fortune will bring us happiness. But after slaving for years to earn it, does having a large bank balance really make us happy? Think of all the other things we could have done with that time. Have we not, in reality, worked for a lifetime for very little benefit?.

2 *Does Increased Sexual Frequency Enhance Happiness* Carnegie Mellon University, 2015. Journal of Economic Behavior & Organization. 116, 206-218.

Whatever ambition we set ourselves and work towards, the reward will be transient. It will not bring us permanent happiness.

Will our pursuit of happiness make us happy?

We find it disgusting to see a drunk staggering and laughing mindlessly, and we inevitably see him as the lowest form of humanity. Yet the drunk believes he is happy, and inevitably repeats the experience. Is he genuinely happy? Or simply dulling his pain?

The phenomenon of extreme pursuit of happiness is widespread among humans. The most common form is gluttony, leading to obesity. Also common are alcoholism and sex or drug addiction. But how can an excessive amount of anything make us happy? By its very nature, an excess is harmful. Eating too much makes us fat, and therefore unhealthy, depriving us of the great gifts that good health brings. Being ill is a great source of unhappiness, which makes gluttony self-defeating.

Whichever form it takes, the extreme pursuit of pleasure cannot lead to happiness. To believe that because being well-fed makes us happy, eating more food on top will make us happier still, is a common fallacy. Sufficiency is a pleasure, but excess leads to misery rather than joy.

Taking advantage of his wealth and good looks, a womanizer spends his time in frivolous pursuit of pleasure. But when his days run out, and he is old and exhausted, what does he have to show for his life? He has not gained any wisdom during his time on earth. He has spent his time talking and thinking about sex. Even the sex did not make him happy, empty as it was of any personal commitment. Couples who share intimacy and a daily life as well as sex gain far more pleasure from the act than he did.

It is obvious that excessive pleasure just jades our appetite, leading to dissatisfaction rather than joy. The best pleasures in life are brief and memorable, morsels to be savored, not guzzled. An enjoyable night out or a party is a temporary relief from the cares of our day, but we cannot expect such enjoyment to be our every day fare.

Rather than searching for endless joy, we should moderate our ambitions, and search for tranquility instead. Happiness does not befit travelers, who must be constantly moving on rather than losing themselves in pleasure. Remember that we are on a journey, searching for life's purpose, and that purpose is not hedonism.

Tranquility is peace of mind, emotional stability and inner satisfaction. Tranquility leaves us in the right frame of mind to enjoy occasional moments of joy. Whereas seeking endless happiness leads to frustration and discontent, because it is reaching for the impossible, seeking tranquility is a much more realistic goal.

The hypothesis of this book is that seeking pleasure does not lead to pleasure; but attaining tranquility is possible, and can be achieved by balancing the five fundamental elements of our lives. These are our finances, our bodies, our relationships, our inner selves and our souls.

Balancing these five comes naturally to us. We do not need to consciously understand how to do it, because if an imbalance occurs, we instinctively move to correct it.

Where do we find tranquility?

On a balcony one summer's day, at the foot of a wooded mountain, we pulled up comfortable chairs and sat admiring the tree filled valley. Rising from it came the scent of jasmine flowers, the twittering of sparrows, and the full throated singing of nightingales. We were with friends, each of us sipping our favorite hot drinks; coffee for one, cocoa for another, Ceylon tea for a third. Our conversation turned to reminiscences from our childhood. We laughed endlessly, each word spoken heavy with mutual care and compassion. Hours passed, feeling like minutes. We wanted the moment to last forever.

This perfect gathering in an idyllic spot with exceptional people may never come again. But if it had lacked one single element, the entire perfection would have been destroyed. If the weather had been cold, and we lacked warm clothes, our pleasure in the company would have been tarnished. We wouldn't have enjoyed drinking tea, or cared about the beautiful scenery or delicious food, if any element had been missing.

The moral of the story is that lacking any of the five equilibriums will prevent us feeling tranquil. If we had been placed in that same setting, but with detested visitors rather than welcome ones, we would not enjoy the jasmine, tea, scenery or nightingales, because we would lack social equilibrium.

If we had felt cold and not had a jacket, we would have lacked physical equilibrium. If we were worrying about being unable to settle an outstanding loan payment, we would have lacked financial equilibrium. We would also then have lacked spiritual equilibrium, which includes the comfort that comes from knowing that all upcoming risks are insured and secure.

These equilibriums must all be in harmony. For only when all the essential elements are in harmony with each other can we enjoy tranquility and satisfaction, and our minds be at rest.

UNIFORMITY OF LIFE

Wanting to understand the workings of the world we live in is intrinsic to our nature, which is why we created science. The social sciences study how human beings relate to one another, trying to understand our behavior in order to explain it. Psychology studies what happens within our minds, while medicine studies what happens within our bodies. Economics is the science that studies our economic activity and finances.

24

It is more important today than ever, as money rules our lives, and our economies grow ever more complex. Chemistry, physics, geology, geometry, and related studies address our environment in all its aspects.

Our academic disciplines are so far reaching and wide ranging today that no one can master them all. Between them, these sciences set out the rules that govern everything that happens in our world. By applying one or more of them, we can explain any event. Anyone who suggests that an event is random, and just a matter of luck, is misguided. All events have causes. If we apply the right science to the event, we will understand its cause.

The belief in random events is therefore an expression of ignorance. Finding an event's cause is always possible if you have sufficient understanding.

The randomness fallacy

We can examine this further. Sometimes we say that a disease strikes "at random". But as we have just discussed, there is no such thing as a random event. What we are really expressing when we say "at random" is that we lack the understanding to isolate the event's cause. If diseases really struck at random, we would never be able to find cures for them. Yet many can now be cured.

Look at smallpox, for example. From killing more than a hundred million children in the twentieth century, it has been eradicated, as confirmed by the World Health Organization. We are also on the verge of eradicating polio, and we can control measles. These successes show that with sufficient understanding, yesterday's "random disease" can be tomorrow's eradicated disease. The only thing that has changed is our understanding. The disease's apparent randomness was always an illusion.

What this demonstrates is that our universe is truly in harmony. Everything has a cause, because it is the equilibrium between competing forces that causes each event.

To control disease and other problems, we simply need to learn more about how these forces compete. And the more we learn, the more orderly things prove to be. Every component of the universe acts in accordance with predetermined scientific rules. When we examine a solid substance under a microscope, we find that its constituent particles act in accordance with the laws of motion and gravity. There is harmony, or equilibrium, between the elements the substance contains. Since particles are not conscious beings, this equilibrium cannot be at their own instigation. So where does it come from?

To understand the greatness and perfection of the universe, we need to understand the rules that govern it. The same applies to our bodies and minds. Scientists delve into our brains, our organs, and our thoughts and instincts, and they discover new knowledge about us and our environment. From these enquiries, we come to see how thoroughly organized our world is.

We too are organized. We live lives full of difficulty and suffering, joy and sadness. We may think that these events happen at random, and that our lives are no more controlled than if we had been locked in a box and are spinning through the air. But in truth, our lives are just as organized as the laws of physics that carry us across space, and the laws of chemistry that gave us ultra-light smartphones and life-saving drugs. To progress in our understanding of our lives, and to learn how to control the apparently random fluctuations in our circumstances, we need to study the laws that govern our lives, just as we have studied physics and chemistry.

Tranquility is in the details

The complexity of our lives confuses some people, while others flee from the sheer weight of information we have to cope with. But learning about the issues we face and understanding them is the best solution. For example, if we have a minor cut on our leg, some people will think it too trivial to worry about. But negligence can obscure the value of important information, and make small details important. If the leg festers, the complications could result in the whole limb being lost. If we treat every issue on its merits, carefully considering whether they are deserving of our time, we will avoid such unnecessary complications.

This applies to everything in our lives. We must care about the details, and be mentally aware of those variables that can disturb our equilibrium and therefore disrupt our tranquility. Awareness, especially self-awareness, is the key to remaining in equilibrium and preserving tranquility. If a single bolt falls off a complex machine, how can we put it back in the correct place if we have not already observed carefully how the machine works?

We do not have to be doctors or medical experts to take good care of our bodies. It is enough to know the basic principles of healthy nutrition, hygiene, and how we function. We do not need to be an expert in ulcers to understand simple steps to avoid them. Like the T.V. quiz *"Who Wants To Be A Millionaire?"* it is not essential to know everything to win life's prizes, but we do need to know how to ask the right questions, and to be observant enough to recognize when bolts are falling off from our machines.

Life is filled with details, and more details, and the details of details, and the details of details of details, all of which hop around like devils — which is perhaps why we say "The devil is in the details;" because it is only when you inquire deeply into the details that a matter's true complexity becomes apparent.

But in one sense the saying is wrong. Going into matters deeply throws up light and truth, not darkness and devilry.

How do we achieve equilibrium?

If you happen to be a good cook, you'd know that it is not necessary for each individual ingredient of a broth to taste good on its own. Some may be bitter, others sour, or sharp. But by combining them in a recipe you achieve a delicious result. The secret is in having a recipe that balances all the constituent elements to achieve a whole that is far better than the individual ingredients. The same applies to all walks of life. A car factory may be greasy and noisy, but from it rolls a succession of perfect, shiny, beautiful machines.

It is possible to achieve balance in our lives, but to do so we need to ask the right questions. Do not ask "How do I make money?" Instead, ask "How do I achieve equilibrium in my monetary affairs?" Because searching for equilibrium reveals the wisest course to follow, no matter what the issue.

Many people focus so much on trying to make money that they sacrifice either social equilibrium or spiritual equilibrium in the process. They help no one, and ignore morality. Take drug dealers, for example; they make money, but they do it by a process that destroys families, and offends both morality and society. Their very existence is a threat to others.

Similarly, the man who makes money but does it at the expense of taking the time to raise his children properly, or looking after his parents, or being attentive to his wife; such a person destroys his social equilibrium.

He is wealthy, but cannot be considered successful. If he neglects important areas of his life and focuses just on one, he is like a student who learns only one subject. He may excel at chemistry, but will fail all his other exams, and will be unfit for the world of work.

If we make equilibrium our goal we will avoid this failure. We will accord each aspect of our life the value it is due, without trampling on the others. We will pursue money only up to the point that it maintains our financial equilibrium. And when our needs are met we will address other areas that require our attention. In this way, we will maintain our internal equilibrium.

Our internal equilibrium can be disturbed in many ways. Worrying about an approaching event, for example fearing for our son when he is going on a journey, will disturb it. When we try to counter this and restore our internal equilibrium, we must do so in a constructive manner. Rather than trying to change our reality to make the danger go away, we should deal rationally with our fears. It would be wrong to try to dissuade our son from travelling, because although this might restore our own equilibrium in the short term, what effect would it have on him? Since the problem lies within our thoughts, it is our thoughts we must change, not his plans. We must therefore find thoughts that can act as a counterweight to our fear. We should remind ourselves that cosseting him is not in his interests, and will make him weak in life. Or if we are religious, we can remind ourselves that God is the keeper, and we should put our trust in him. In these ways we can restore the equilibrium of our mind.

And so it is with all our equilibriums. Reading on, we will learn together how to monitor our scales and maintain balance in all things.

Do you accept the challenge?

But do not read further until two essential points are clear in your mind.

One: Take on board that our lives are disciplined and balanced, and that any seeming randomness of events is an illusion. We imagine events to be random because we are too small to see the wider frame; and we frequently fail to use what intelligence we have to analyze life's complexities.

Two: You must accept the challenge implicit in this book. Most challenges in life involve achieving a goal or overcoming a problem. But the challenge in this book is on a higher plane. To understand and apply the concept of equilibrium is to bring our social, physical, financial, psychological and spiritual aims within reach. It is not a challenge limited by time or scope. Its impact is to rebuild ourselves in a radical way, to raise our minds and our spirits to the highest heights, to pursue unending improvement; because only with our minds, bodies and lives in equilibrium can we reach our true potential. Once we understand the strength that comes from attaining equilibrium within ourselves, our dreams and ambitions can soar.

A balanced life

Equilibrium is not a single objective, it is a group of balanced dimensions that once achieved makes our path straight and our goals clear. Just as a successful student must master all his courses before graduating, so we must attain equilibrium in all the essential elements that constitute our life. We cannot achieve equilibrium while leaving parts of our life unbalanced.

Moving down the scale, the same applies to each individual dimension of our lives. Achieving equilibrium in our health means that all aspects of our health must be in harmony, from our weight to our diet and fitness. And achieving internal equilibrium results from balancing our thoughts, needs, emotions and everything that passes through our brains. The same principle applies to our social equilibrium, spiritual equilibrium and financial equilibrium. They each require every aspect to be in harmony.

Chapter 2: Navigate life

THE FIVE EQUILIBRIUMS

ONE: FINANCIAL EQUILIBRIUM

Most people would say that financial equilibrium is synonymous with financial security; the greater our savings, the closer we are to financial equilibrium. But is this right? How far should we go in our search for financial security? And where should we draw the line and say "That is enough?"

Our needs in terms of savings, liquid assets and property are relative. A poor man may feel that he is doing well if he has sufficient to feed and clothe his family, and put a little aside. Whereas a rich man would view the same amount as derisory, and patently insufficient. But as our wealth grows, our horizons change and our "needs" expand. What satisfied us yesterday is insufficient today, and what we aspire to today will be insufficient tomorrow. This is because avarice is intrinsic to human nature.

For this reason no amount of money is ever "sufficient". We are always chasing more than we have. But this ambition is destructive of the rest of our lives, and denies us equilibrium in other areas. We waste our talent and energy on a goal that is always receding from our grasp, a mirage that can never be reached. Like Tantalus in the Underworld, our striving for money will never reach fruition, because it is our money-making instinct that drives us rather than actual need.

Imagine a vampire, driven by a lust for blood, but unable to satisfy that lust because the more it drinks the greater its thirst. Or a rabid dog, biting wildly, not out of hunger but out of a mad rage that compels it to bite. In the same way, humans chase money, not because we need it, but because our instincts drive us remorselessly. A love of possessions feeds the greed inside us, driving us to hoard our wealth far beyond the point at which it is useful.

We need to understand this fact, and act on it. As it is impossible to achieve financial satisfaction, we must not squander our energies trying. We must set adequate targets, and then re-prioritize our energy to achieve equilibrium in other spheres.

The essence of financial equilibrium

We can picture financial equilibrium as Libra holding up two scales. The first scale holds our short-term benefit; the second, our long-term benefit. Equilibrium is achieved when the two are level.

Short term benefits might include spending a monthly budget to meet our expenses and enjoy a certain amount of consumption for pleasure. Long term benefits might include savings, or investing time and effort to improve our earning power to change our situation from being poor to rich; thereby postponing consumption into the future.

Financial Equilibrium involves balancing these two. If we spend too much on short term consumption, we will stay poor. But if we look too much to the future, our vision becomes clouded. We then deny ourselves any pleasure, thinking that there is no point in enjoying ourselves to day because until we reach our long term goals we will never be happy, and that any pleasure we have today will necessarily be incomplete. This may cause us to save too much and consume too little, and keep us from achieving equilibrium.

Depending on our situation, there are many variables to consider when addressing the question of financial equilibrium. On the one hand, helping our siblings financially when they are in need, or helping fund their education, may hold us back and hinder our own path to prosperity. But on the other, failing to help them would create tension within the family.

Age is another important factor. The young tend to waste money, whereas the old tend to save too much, when it should really be the other way around. Postponing consumption when we are young will not harm us, as we have many years ahead in which to catch up. But if we are old, saving more than we have to may cause unnecessary hardship to ourselves and our families.

For the old, money can also be used to help us achieve equilibrium in other areas of our lives. Philanthropy, and generosity with money generally, open access to people's hearts, helping us achieve social equilibrium. While donations to charity help us achieve spiritual equilibrium, and to purify our souls.

The opportunity to achieve these benefits makes saving in old age especially inappropriate.

Obstacles to Financial Equilibrium

1. Setting unrealistic ambitions

We all share the ambition of amassing great wealth, and many of us work extremely hard in the hope of achieving it. But how many actually succeed? High ambitions feed our instinct to reach for excellence, glory and exceptional power, leading us to become infected with greed. By committing ourselves to excessively ambitious goals, and devoting our energy to chasing them, we submit to being harnessed and ridden like beasts of burden in a never ending race. Rather than helping us achieve financial equilibrium, such ambitions make it impossible.

The right goals to set are ones that do not harm our other equilibriums. Wanting to expand our wealth and possessions is natural. It is not bad in itself, as long as we keep the ambition in perspective, and understand that our ownership of possessions is transient. In time we will move on, and everything we build will perish. We will then understand the truth, that our "ownership" was only temporary, and that our other equilibriums – our physical, social and spiritual equilibriums, also need nurturing, and are equally worth investing in. If we set financial ambitions that are too high, we will squander the thought and energy that should be devoted to these other important areas.

2. Laziness

It's not easy to find a job we enjoy doing day after day, and the search may require considerable commitment. But it is worthwhile, for there is a perfect occupation for each of us. Once we find that ideal occupation we will also find the enthusiasm needed to work hard and to excel. The greatest obstacle we face in this search is internal doubt. Doubt that we can succeed, and fear of trying lest we fail.

Some people are so scared of failing that they prefer to accept being poor rather than attaining the wealth they are capable of. Striving to attain our potential requires us to try and fail, and to learn from our mistakes and failures. These are things that the lazy or unmotivated shrink from.

3. Ignorance

a) Ignorance of the cost -v- benefit of learning

Gaining knowledge is the key to our advancement, whereas being satisfied with what we know is relaxing in the arms of ignorance. We must ensure that we stay up to date with developments in the craft or a skill that we use to earn our living, either by talking to other practitioners or by following the profession's news. Doing this assiduously will keep us competitive and well-informed. Sometimes great advantages can accrue from small pieces of knowledge. By staying up to date we are well positioned to spot opportunities, increase our income, and improve our prospects of reaching the top in our field.

We may be keen on the benefits that learning brings, but unwilling to make the sacrifices it requires, or to take the risk that investing in knowledge implies. Perhaps we paint houses for a living, and our income is too low to let us save much. We then hear of a course that would teach us new skills that would improve our value as a painter and increase our income. But we would need to take out a five month loan to pay for the course. Should we take the risk?

Some people would hesitate, being reluctant to go beyond their comfort zone. But gaining knowledge and expanding our horizons are important. The course will introduce us to new techniques, and to successful painters from whom we can learn. As well as the formal course we will be able to exchange ideas, share skills, and gain new ways of thinking. The interchange of ideas may stimulate our own creativity, and increase the quality of our work. In time we may become sought after for the quality of our work, and increase our prices, and take on staff to meet our expanding demand. From small beginnings we may become an employer with a company that accumulates capital and makes us rich.

There are many such success stories, and they all depend on making sacrifices to gain the knowledge that will help us reach our goals.

b) Ignorance of wealth facts

Our hands are often closed when we are born, yet no one would think to open them and look to see what we are holding, because we come into this world with nothing. But when we leave the world we have possessions to bequeath.

Working to the best of our ability and waiting patiently for the rewards will in time bring us wealth. But envying the wealth of others will destroy our patience, breed dissatisfaction, and impede our path to financial equilibrium.

4. Thinking too much about wealth

We obtain wealth by hard work and diligence, and as part of this process it is natural to spend time thinking about money. But we should not allow our thoughts to become too focused on money. If we are facing a difficult financial problem, then by all means concentrate on solving it. But constantly using our mental energy to search out ways of making money is wasting our brains, which were not designed to focus on just one area of our lives.

We can best expand our wealth by applying the popular formula of Barito (20-80); that is to say that we should work our bodies 80% of our working time, and work our brains 20% of our free time. Anything more will lead to an imbalance in our lives, because our finances are only one of the essential dimensions of our life, and financial equilibrium is only one of the five equilibriums we need to strive for. Putting all our eggs in one basket can only lead to disaster.

5. Entrapment of values and principles

John has been dreaming about his big project for years. But he has had difficulty finding a good business partner. His first partner backed out, and it took months of searching to find a replacement. Then this second partner backed out at the last moment, and when John found another replacement, a problem arose concerning one of the articles the new partner inserted into the draft contract. John couldn't agree to it, because it contradicted his ethical principles. So he was faced with a terrible dilemma; should he pursue his project at the expense of his principles?

Some opportunities in life are nothing but traps. Few people would resist the temptation once they have tasted the excitement of getting the project underway. But once we let ourselves be drawn in, we will be sullied for the rest of our lives. Ethics exist to steer us away from such temptations, for it is important that we maintain high moral standards in our search for wealth. Wealth is the lure that too often detaches us from morality.

TWO: PHYSICAL EQUILIBRIUM

Our parents nourish and nurture our bodies through childhood, but in time we must assume these responsibilities ourselves. To do this, we need to learn how our bodies work, and monitor both what we eat and our health. The two must be considered side by side, because although disease can come from the air we breathe and water we drink, in today's world it is the food we eat that is the greatest source of disease. Our cells renew and replenish themselves with the food we consume, and we literally become what we have eaten.

The keys to physical equilibrium

Achieving physical equilibrium requires us to understand our bodies, so that we can focus on what benefits them and avoid what harms them. Awareness of our bodies and an understanding of their mechanics are therefore the keys to physical equilibrium.

Understanding the mechanics of our bodies lets us judge which actions or substances will harm them, and which will strengthen them. We can then appreciate why exercise in important, why certain foods overstress our organs, why poor housing or a bad environment or even certain clothing can negatively impact our proper functions.

Awareness of our bodies allows us to make informed decisions, and to predict and gauge their effect. Without this awareness we are ignorant, and cannot understand how we will be affected by the things we do, the things we eat, and the things we encounter. But when we light the candle of knowledge, it lights up the hole of disease that people in the past fell into, and we realize that we are in danger of repeating their mistakes.

Obstacles to physical equilibrium

Physical equilibrium shares a characteristic with all the other equilibriums, in that it comes to us naturally. We do not need to learn how to achieve it, we simply need to allow our bodies to fulfill their natural functions. It is only when we interfere with these natural processes that we impede our progress towards equilibrium. When this occurs, we must search for and identify the obstruction preventing our body from maintaining equilibrium. Such obstacles can come from many angles, including:

1. Needs becoming goals

There is a saying that we should "eat to live," rather than "live to eat". Often, it is the reversal of these two that prevents us maintaining equilibrium. The natural enjoyment of food transforms into gluttony, turning an important need into a vice. The same applies to our other important functions. The need to mate and produce offspring becomes transformed into licentiousness, and the need to secure safe housing and clothes to keep us warm become pride, materialism and greed. Having been transformed from needs to self-gratifying goals, these vices then take over our lives.

Understanding our instincts and desires, and being able to meet them in a wholesome way, are very different from indulging in excess. To an extent it is natural to indulge more than we strictly need, but gorging on food and elevating sexual satisfaction into an obsession degrade us, turning us from humans into animals. By indulging our bodily needs to excess we are ignoring our other needs, and the higher functions of our minds. Chasing sexual gratification and fighting to dominate and control are animal functions, and if they become our only motivations we are indeed no better than animals.

2. Slavishly following bad habits

Many of our health habits are formed in our youth. This includes our favorite foods, and the way in which we treat our bodies. But as youths our minds were still maturing, and even after we become adults, we often fail to correct the errors that we adopted when young. Some of us still eat meat on a daily basis, as we did when we were younger, even though we are in our fifties and understand that we need to change our diet to include vegetables and salad, or face the risk of colon cancer which lurks just around the corner. Some of us are volatile in our employment, jumping from job to job, without learning a healthy and stable way to manage our career. While others are in their fifties or sixties yet fail to exercise, even though their bodies are getting old and need the strengthening and repair that a daily walk could help supply. They may not yet be complaining of any illness, but their internal organs are like cars that have been running for fifty or sixty years, and are in need of care.

These examples are just a few to illustrate the many ways in which we mismanage our bodies. There are too many faults to list them all, but ignorance about what we eat, drink and do with our bodies is the biggest obstacle to physical equilibrium. Stopping, thinking, and reconsidering how we treat our bodies, and learning more about them, are essential if we want to achieve and sustain physical equilibrium.

3. Food and drink

Food and drink fortify us, and are essential to our health. But paradoxically, they also throw up some of the greatest obstacles to our health. It is impossible to reach physical equilibrium without being aware of the risk they represent, and the need to refrain from consuming them in excess. It is also essential to be aware of the danger that many of them bring, for not all foods are safe. When our cells renew they are influenced by the kinds of food and drink we have consumed; food is literally the raw material that builds us. It is only if we choose our raw materials wisely that they will strengthen, rather than weaken us.

The kinds of food and drinks that we like are different from the kinds our bodies like. We could even picture ourselves and our bodies as two separate systems, each with its own priorities. We enjoy sweet foods, while our digestive systems enjoy vegetables and salad. We generally like meat and fat, but they are exhausting to our digestive systems, kidneys and arteries. Extending the analogy, we often prefer laziness, but our bodies enjoy movement. Below are the most important issues that arise from neglecting what we eat and drink:

A. Not investigating the quality of our food

Healthy food is not convenience food, we therefore need to seek it out. It is often more expensive, and takes more effort to find, but making the effort is worthwhile because we are what we eat. Poor nutrition inevitably leads us to many diseases.

There is so much for us to learn about food, and it can bring so many benefits. But only if we have the knowledge to choose wisely. Consider honey. Some honey is beneficial, containing much more than just sugar. Good honey can be a magical ingredient that boosts our immune system. While other honey is mass produced, from bees fed sugar solution, and gives us little more than sweetness that we like but do not need. How do we know which honey is good, and which is not? Finding the best honey requires experience, knowledge, research. And in the end, we will pay an exceptional price for an exceptional spoon of honey.

B. Neglecting water

If you have a headache, pour two and half liters of water and begin to drink it slowly. Note how your headache lessens. If you are surprised, remember that water is the elixir of life. It maintains the clarity of our complexion, and the function of our internal organs. Nearly 70% of our body is water. Running short is one of the habits most damaging to the body, and a common obstruction that impedes physical equilibrium.

4. Violating our nature

Violating our nature inevitably obstructs our body's balance. This violation can come in three forms: Departing from our animal nature , overusing our brains, and failing to differentiate between the exception and the rule.

A. Departing from our animal nature

Our bodies have many animal characteristics, and many properties in common with those of animals. This is why testing medicines on animals is often useful. If we violate the physical side of this animal nature, it makes us susceptible to disease. For example, if we are lazy and avoid exercise, it lays us open to illness. We were not designed to sit down all day, we were designed to walk about and exert ourselves. And we need this exertion to stay fit, just as cows and sheep that are grazed in fields are less susceptible to disease than ones locked up in barns.

When cows were fed the meat of their own species, the result was mad cow disease. The disease outbreak began in Europe and resulted in the slaughter of thousands of infected cows around the world. It only ended when measures to stop the feeding of cow protein to cows were instituted. Such a practice was bound to be harmful, because cows are not meant to eat meat, let alone the meat of their own species. Violating the cows' nature led to this deadly disease – which also killed some humans who ate infected meat – and demonstrated that violating any species' nature is harmful. But have we learnt the lesson?

To achieve equilibrium we must respect our physical nature. Instead, we eat manufactured, colored sweets with flavors that cannot not be natural, but come from laboratories and factories that smell of toxic fumes. How many of us stop to wonder where the candy's gold and silver colors that dazzle our kids come from? Do we ever wonder whether our digestive system can deal with them? Or what strain it suffers in digesting them? Or whether they produce harmful by-products? Given the junk that we eat, when our doctor tells us that we have colon cancer, do we have the right to be surprised?

Our houses have turned into enclosed boxes of steel and concrete with little daylight. Do we ask ourselves before moving in whether perhaps we need sunlight? We clean the floors with manufactured chemicals and paint the walls with artificial dyes, all of which are unnatural and alien to our bodies. Our bodies demand houses of natural material, with wooden floors, and windows that let in the sun. Natural materials are healthier and gentler. They breathe better, are warmer in winter and cooler in summer. Wood once grew and multiplied, it shared the spark of life that we enjoy; it fits with our nature, for it was once a living thing. But concrete and metal are things of the dead.

Cotton clothes are also gentler than synthetic, for cotton too is a natural product that lived and grew as we do. Who has ever heard of a man or woman with cotton sensitivity? Yet we are never sure how our bodies will react to synthetic materials, or the harm they cause us.

B. Overusing our brains

The brain is an organ just like the heart, kidneys and liver. Like these other organs, it has a natural equilibrium of its own and can suffer from overuse. Our brain needs working time and resting time. It recovers from its exertions when we sleep. If we are constantly awake it cannot repair itself, and it suffers. Permanent sadness is not good for it either. Both fatigue and sadness sap its vitality. [3]Research shows that fatigue weakens our immune system too.

In fact sleep is an essential activity just like eating or breathing. The world of sleep is unfathomably complex. We are only just beginning to understand its full impact, which extends deep into our lives. Science is starting to shine a light on this fascinating world, like a research submarine exploring the depths of the oceans but with lamps as yet too feeble to penetrate far into the gloom.

What we do know is that sleeping charges our mental and physical batteries. An occasional lack of sleep may not harm our bodies. But if we run short of sleep repeatedly we struggle to remain alert, and long term sleep deficiency soon harms our productivity and our health. Adequate sleep is therefore an essential requirement for maintaining all our equilibriums.

---

3 http://www.webmd.com/sleep-disorders/features/immune-system-lack-of-sleep

Our brains can be harmed by negative thoughts, too. When these impulses dominate our minds, forcing our brains to focus on the negative aspects of our surroundings, they result in depression, in which we see only the bad side of the people around us. Studies have shown that if this persists it can damage our brain's capacity to feel positive, for it was not wired to cope with unrelenting negativity. To avoid this we must endeavor to relax, and take a balanced approach to the way we use our minds.

Emptiness is the worse attribute we can ascribe to a person; someone who is empty is trivial. But a certain degree of emptiness can be beneficial, rescuing our minds from the illness that follows from too much intensity. Emptying our minds lets us escape, albeit briefly, from the pressure of our daily existence, and allows us to view our lives from a wider perspective. In seeing things from the outside looking in we can sometimes spot the mistakes we are making, and identify ways to improve. Emptying our minds for a short time each day, by pursuing a hobby, playing with our children, or jogging, may be the most healthful habit for our busy brains.

C. Exception and the rule

Failing to differentiate between the exception and the rule will violate our nature, Our bodies have the capacity to repair themselves. Injuries heal, colds fade and disappear. But illnesses do not pack their bags and leave just because their vacation is over; they leave because our bodies resist their presence and drive them away. This self-healing ability can cope with a limited amount of pesticide contaminated food, unnatural, synthetic clothing, or impure air and water; but if the burden we place on our bodies is too high they begin losing ground in the battle for health.

Therefore it is important to know our body's capacity, and to be able to differentiate between the exception and the rule. Taking an occasional sip of a canned drink without checking what is in it may not do us much harm. We can rely on the basic protection that comes from the drink being legally available, and assume that had it been extremely harmful it would have been banned by the state. But if we are going to drink it every day we need to inquire more deeply into its ingredients. Does it contain preservatives, colorings, artificial flavors or sweeteners? If it is laden with sugar or chemicals, we should stay away.

The same principle applies to our need for exercise. Failing to exercise for a week or so will not kill us. But avoiding exercise long term is very harmful.

There are many other health habits, foods and drinks that we need to view in this light. The body is flexible and resilient enough to cope with them on the odd occasion; but if we indulge too often, or let our defenses down on a daily basis, we risk suffering harm.

5. Not knowing how to deal with illness

Our bodies resist illness as a matter of course, waging a constant battle between our organs and systems on the one hand, and pathogens on the other. The fact that we do not see this battle taking place in no way diminishes its importance. Nor should we underestimate the toll this battle can take on our body's resources. Therefore we should equip it with the weapons it needs to win the fight. At the same time, we should have faith in our body's resilience, which means not actively intervening unless it asks for help.

Times do arise when help is needed. Sometimes it is enough just to keep warm, and to rest. But if an illness persists, we need medical intervention.

A. Understanding what our body is saying

If our bodies are feeling neglected they call out, demanding rest, sleep or food. Sometimes they send their message through the medium of pain. Whatever language they use, we must learn to recognize these messages and respond. Pain in particular is an important message that we should not ignore. It acts as an early warning device that precedes catastrophe, and taking pain killers may hinder us from hearing its message clearly. Back pain, for example, is a warning to correct our posture, lifting technique, or the way we sit. Unpleasant as it might be, pain alerts us to our mistakes and warns us to correct them.

When our body sends a message the right response is to deal with the problem it has highlighted. Ignoring the message is dangerous, as it leaves the underlying issue unresolved. If we are hungry, but choose to ignore that hunger without considering the state of our body and its nutritional needs, we risk causing ourselves harm. We therefore have to learn to differentiate between hunger pangs that are urgent, and represent a real need for food; and feelings of hunger that are really prompted by gluttony, and the expectation of a meal at six o'clock whether we need it or not.

Awareness of our state of health is key to understanding our needs, and the signals our body sends. Some of these can be safely ignored. Resting every time our body asks for rest may not be wise. Rest is important when we are sick, or exhausted, but we do need to challenge our body with exercise to the point of being tired. So we need to differentiate between genuine exhaustion, and the body's natural inclination to laziness. Relaxation has its place, but many other things in life are also important.

B. Getting to the truth of medical data

Blindly accepting the validity of published medical information will harm our chances of attaining of physical equilibrium. Here is a good example. The conventional view based on controlled studies was that consuming 60mg per day of Vitamin C could help overcome signs of aging and many diseases. This level was established in 1980. But a 1999 paper[4] questioned the adequacy of this 60mg level, and said it was based on incomplete and inaccurate data. Instead, it proposed a daily intake of 120mg a day. The new report also noted that taking supplements of Vitamin C did not produce the improved outcomes expected, in relation to heart disease, and produced conflicting results in relation to cataract prevention. In light of this, would it have been wise to rely on the original research?

Putting scientific theories into context is essential to judging their validity. Today, we know a thousand times more than scientists knew a hundred years ago; but a hundred years into the future scientists will regard us as utterly ignorant. If a piece of "knowledge" contradicts common sense, or flies in the face of the plain evidence of our senses, we should treat it with caution. The chances are that at some point in the future, a new piece of research will come along to disprove it.

We should also consider how a particular piece of research has been funded. There are many different motives for funding research, and if a billion dollar pharmaceutical corporation funds research that happens to end up supporting their products, we should be cautious about taking it at face value.

---

4 JAMA, April 21, 1999—Vol 281, No. 15 1415

Some people seek treatment for their illnesses in the same way as they take a malfunctioning car to be serviced. They do not care about the reasons behind the illness, or the nature of the treatment; they just want their body to be fixed so that they can carry on using it as normal. But treating your body in this way, without trying to understand causes and effects, opens you up to further illness in the future. Illnesses are smart, and to keep ahead of them we need to understand them. By understanding them, we build the strongest possible defense against letting them recur. And although it is wise to listen to what doctors tell us, given their training and experience, they are not infallible. They suffer from human error like the rest of us, and they cannot understand our symptoms as well as we do. Our brains are in constant touch with our bodies, and are therefore uniquely well placed to understand the details of our condition. By using this understanding, we build the strongest possible defense against doctors' human error.

Consider a drug which, as a side effect, causes a rash on our skin. Would we realize that the rash is coming from the drug? And if we do, should we immediately stop using it, or should we wait until we see our doctor? Or consider an illness that is discovered years after we contracted it. In the meantime, our doctor has been trying to treat its symptoms with one medicine after another. But all attempts fail, because the doctor was not aware of the true nature of the disease.

Doctors treat according to their understanding. But medical knowledge is necessarily imperfect, so many treatments will fail. Being aware that there is a lot doctors do not know, and that there is much knowledge yet to be discovered, may rescue us from becoming a lab rat as they struggle with one failed treatment after another, and pronounce us an 'interesting case', and share our fascinating history at conferences and in medical publications. Which is why uncritical reliance on our doctor's knowledge may prevent us reaching physical equilibrium.

C.Ignoring a healthy diet

A healthy diet is one that shuns foods that harm our bodies and therefore avoids making us ill. The vast majority of illnesses are caused by a bad diet, and can be prevented by a good one. We grumble about having to avoid foods that harm us, and many people eat badly then try to compensate by taking pills and supplements. But the benefits of a healthy diet cannot be reproduced by supplements or pills.

We need to follow cures that strike at the roots of the disease. If we are suffering from a sore throat, we must avoid cold drinks. If we have an upset stomach, we should avoid fat and sweets. And if we have gastric acid, we should abstain from tomatoes and other foods that cause acidity. If we have a skin rash, staying away from foods that cause rashes is often enough to make it disappear. And if we are unable to find out which food is responsible, we should stay away from all foods that may be causing it, one after the other, and see which helps.

These are but a few examples of a principle that is fundamental to our health. Diet is the oldest, yet still the most effective, treatment to take care of our bodies. We must remember that we can either control our diet, or accept being ill. These are the only two choices.

D. Forgetting that food is also medicine

It is not simply a matter of avoiding foods that are harmful. Food can also be an essential part of the cure for some diseases. Many diseases are caused by it, yet many diseases can be prevented by it. There are too many examples of the relationship between food and health to name them here, but a little research will quickly find them. Such research is in itself beneficial, for the relationship between food and our bodies is one we need to learn about.

E. Abandoning herbal medication

Our bodies are astonishingly complex machines. Science's ambition of unraveling their mysteries, and understanding how particular foods affect us, has led to intensive research. This in turn has brought us an unprecedentedly deep understanding of our bodies' functions. Yet there is still so much more to learn.

Let's imagine our bodies as villas filled with corridors of dark rooms. As food passes through these rooms it is digested.

Scientists are forever trying to throw light into these dark rooms, to catch glimpses of the mystical processes taking place within. Sometimes they succeed, and learn something new. Other times they fail, and our bodies keep their secrets.Sometimes they half succeed, and can see dim shadows moving within the room, but not make out all the details.

At present we know comparatively little about the way in which most individual foods interact with our bodies. The same applies to most medicines. We know a little of what transpires when we take a substance, but much remains hidden. So treat with skepticism any advice about what you should avoid, and what you should eat every day; or which pills are safe to take, and which are not. Because our knowledge is so slim.

When we medicate with herbs on the other hand, we are taking substances that we understand. And when we take what we know and understand, we have more chance of predicting how our bodies will be affected. Unlike synthetic drugs, manufactured for just a few years and hastily tested before being sold, herbal medicines have been used for millennia. We have had the time needed to understand their strengths and weaknesses. Research into the effects of a new drug is brief and unreliable; it may be pronounced safe today, and dangerous tomorrow when new evidence comes to light. Today's wonder drug may one day be found skulking in one of those dark rooms and wreaking havoc.

Herbs are not completely free of danger. But their drawbacks are better understood, because we have used them for so long. Many herbal practitioners are deeply learned in their craft, having studied no less intensively than a medical doctor. Their benefits have been widely experienced, with many people's lives enriched by the experience of herbs that saved them from needing manufactured drugs, and kept their immune systems strong.

THREE: SOCIAL EQUILIBRIUM

A life without love for others has no meaning. If we cannot find someone to celebrate our successes with, how can these moments be truly happy? And if we are alone when we face adversity, who will console us, and soften life's harsh blows?

Our lives are far more beautiful and more fulfilled, as well as safer and more balanced, if there are people around us who we love, and whose love and support we receive in return. The emotions generated by love are more than pretty flowers that decorate our lives; they are an urgent need. An absence of such emotions consigns us to social emptiness. Our need to connect with people we love is greater than our need for food, drink and shelter. To exist without this social connection is more harmful than we can imagine. The loneliness that comes from isolation may turn our feelings to hatred, misery and hopelessness. In such a state, we cannot hope to achieve equilibrium.

Although friends are essential, our need for them should not be allowed to run wild. Friendship brings responsibilities. Having too many friends will create more responsibilities than we can cope with; on the other hand, having too few will leave our needs unsatisfied. A friendship must be cultivated and nurtured, in the same way that we nurture a young tree when we plant it. If it is not watered with a steady stream of mutual contact and pleasantries, a friendship will die.

But having too few friends is unhealthy too. There is always a risk of friends leaving, or becoming too busy or distracted to continue engaging. If we have just a few friends and some disappear, we will be left short, and lonely. When we lose friends it is difficult to make more. Friendship cannot be bought, and nor can we obtain friends, as we did in our childhood, by approaching people and asking "Do you want to be my friend?"

Without friends our need for social participation is unsatisfied. This runs contrary to our social nature, and undermines our equilibrium. For there is an urgent "social" need in all of us to share what we know with others, to help and be helped. There is even a center in our brain that requires us to share our lives with companions. When this need is being met our brain sends positive signals to the rest of our body, which then works harmoniously, making it easier for us to achieve balance in all our equilibriums. Our lives are more satisfying, and we draw closer to the permanent inner stability we seek.

But a person who is alone for too long falls prey to negative thoughts, and the resulting social imbalance will prevent that person caring effectively for their financial, psychological, spiritual and physical needs.

The belief that life is for sharing drives us to search for suitable people to share it with. When we find a potential partner, if we are truly suitable we will show them sincere love, and they will reciprocate with a love that is equally honest. Such love will be demonstrated in our thoughts and our actions, and in the thoughts and actions of our partner, for the human brain instinctively responds to emotions by reciprocating. This virtuous cycle will engender a closeness and intimacy that activates centers of positive emotion in our brain.

Our struggle to make friends and find loved ones should be pursued with the same intensity as our struggle to make money. Anyone who cares more for making money than for nurturing friendships will inevitably find that, later in their lives, they will be surrounded by people who care only for the money they have amassed and not for their friendship. Their life will be devoid of love or genuine warmth.

It is our social and emotional equilibriums that give our lives meaning. It is a strange paradox that people who lack money are often more open minded, more at peace, and closer to being genuinely satisfied in life, than those who have great wealth. It is also an observation worth noting that such people are more trusted by their friends, and can turn to them readily for loans in times of need. Although they move in circles of modest wealth, the bonds of friendship and love they share make it common for them to trust each other with what are, relative to their income, very large sums.

Some people neglect the search for social equilibrium. They assume that once they have amassed sufficient money, they will find people to love them. This may be true. But becoming rich is never a certainty, and if they fail, they will end up with neither money nor companionship. It is not surprising to learn that research[5] into loneliness shows that it is more harmful than smoking fifteen cigarettes in a day.

Our social need is not simply for people to laugh with and enjoy companionship, but for people who genuinely care about us from the bottom of their hearts; for these are our real friends. They worry about our health when we get sick, and encourage us when we stumble. When we are hurt, they are hurt, and when we are worried, they are worried, for they truly care about the things that affect us. And if we seek a loan from them, they lend without reservation. In return, we reciprocate by caring for them and their interests, and by caring for whatever they hold dear.

If we find that we do not have such friendships, and we cannot find anyone to reciprocate our love, the fault lies with us, not them. Perhaps we are not sufficiently thoughtful or considerate about the way we behave towards others.*

*My article *"Your Ride In Your Journey"* published by *Al-Rai Kuwaiti* newspaper on 25th April 2012, clarifies this further.

5 Statistics New Zealand (2013). Loneliness in New Zealand: Findings from the 2010 NZ General Social Survey. Available from www.stats.govt.nz.

The Heart of Social Equilibrium

Before finding equilibrium in our social lives, we must first find a partner for whom we truly care. Sharing our life, being motivated to make sacrifices, valuing the welfare and happiness of our partner above our own, and caring for the things they hold dear, are essential prerequisites to our own equilibrium. Maintaining such a relationship is only possible if we show consideration, and if we genuinely take their interests to heart. Reaching social equilibrium is simply a matter of loving someone with genuine devotion. Then they will have no option but to reciprocate.

Obstacles to Social Equilibrium

1. Our emotions

When a disagreement arises between us and someone we know well, it can become personally charged. A wave of emotion batters the relationship, and hinders us from dealing rationally with the issue. The strength of this emotional wave varies. Sometimes it is a short-lived but angry outburst, like a destructive tsunami that dashes all logic aside. Other times it can be a rolling ocean swell that cannot be contained, and continues swirling for days.

Emotions are powerful forces that disrupt us all at one time or another, and we don't always recognize the effect they are having on our reason. We should always focus on issues, and avoid letting emotions take control. When someone pushes ahead of us in a queue, it is our emotions that prevent us from controlling our words. But controlling our response, choosing neutral words and not raising our voice, are all essential if we are to deal with the problem rationally.

Avoiding displaying anger signals is difficult, because our posture, expression, and our need to be heard all send negative messages to the target of our anger. Even if we restrain ourselves from cutting them off when they speak, our eyes flash with an unmistakable intensity and our voice is filled with resentment.

To genuinely control our emotions we must first be able to pardon the person's behavior. If we give them the benefit of the doubt rather than automatically assuming that they are culpable, we have more chance of responding calmly, and of sorting the issue out without tempers flaring. That does mean that we must back down, just that we should minimize the risk of confrontation by being calm and reasonable. By pardoning them we will restore our emotional equilibrium, and if we then criticize them we will do it in a constructive and restrained way.

A pacifist who never gets angry is no closer to equilibrium than someone who is always angry, because balance requires both a measure of anger and of calmness. Sometimes a display of anger – whether real or not – can demonstrate a strength of feeling that prevents our rights being trampled on. If anger is not triggered by an unjust violation, it will signal a green light for others to take advantage of us.

63

When we are good at dealing with strangers, it is easier to gain their confidence. Once we have that we can readily make them our friends, because good people are rare coins, and everyone wants to own one.

Real life is more complex than our example of getting angry in the queue. Someone who gets fired from their job is bound to fall prey to strong emotions, including a fear of falling into poverty, anger towards the person who made the decision, and anxiety about their prospects. But they must ignore emotions tied to the past, and concentrate on planning for the future.

2. Ignoring feedback

Major corporations spend millions of dollars to get feedback from consumers. They encourage feedback on websites, send out emails, even offer incentives, all in the hope of learning what their customers like and dislike. They do this because they know that criticism helps them improve.

We can also improve personally if we welcome others' criticism, and treat it constructively. But our emotions often react against it. When this happens we are shooting the messenger and ignoring the value within the message.

Sometimes we become upset about advice not because it is bad advice, or because we are reluctant to improve, but because we dislike being corrected by a particular person. We then fall into the trap many have fallen into; confusing advice with insult. This false link must be eradicated from our brain. Like a computer virus, it reduces our efficiency. How can someone who takes offence at learning hope to improve?

We don't need to spend millions on getting feedback, all we need is to be receptive to good advice. If we sense that someone is uncomfortable, our question should be: "I'm sorry, I think I've offended you, which I honestly did not mean to do. Do you mind clarifying how I can make things better?"

If they answer, the information they provide will give us a clearer vision of ourselves, and help us understand how others see us.

If there are people in our orbit who fail to care about us, the cause is because we do not care about them. It is not the other way around. If we showed a sincere interest in their welfare, they could not avoid returning the interest. Good social skills allow us to choose suitable friends from among our circle of acquaintances, and to draw these people closer to us; but to keep those who are unsuitable at a safe distance.

Marginalizing family

After years of marriage, some men fail to appreciate – or simply ignore - that their wives know them well enough to spot signs of a lack of interest, or of being distant. A wife is very receptive to a diminishing of her husband's love, and can tell just by looking into his eyes, or the way he holds his hands, or the expression that plays across his face, maybe without him even knowing he is doing it. Given the intuitive nature of many women, they will pick up on and probe such signs. If they think that they have lost the husband they love, they will feel there is little left to lose, and will react harshly. War then breaks out.

If we do not find the time for our family, they will rightly feel neglected. Our children will know they are being marginalized, and because they are close to us they have the ability to hurt us, causing us to lose our social equilibrium. This equilibrium is founded on the rock of family life. When our home is a stable, healthy environment, it is a paradise. When it is toxic it can be hell, and we must then dwell in its fire.

3. Searching for a pattern

Our relations with people vary. We trust some people, we distrust others. We treat some well, we treat others more harshly, because what works for Jim does not work for Bob. People are different, and finding a single rule that applies to all our dealings with them is difficult.

We cannot say that from now on we will trust nobody, just because one person has let us down. Nor can we be offensive to all strangers, just because someone has taken advantage of our good nature in the past.

Drawing conclusions from our experiences, and trying to formulate rules based on those experiences, is reasonable. But we have to remember that every rule has an exception. In this case, people are the exception, and if we try rigorously to govern our social relations by predetermined rules, we will end up lonely introverts. Searching for reliable patterns works in other areas of life, but people are too complex to fit into set categories.

4. Failing to acquire social skills

Social skills are the safety systems that let us negotiate society's tortuous byways without crashing or causing anyone any harm. They are the navigation equipment that bring us close to potential friends in safety, and makes it easier to enrich one another's lives. And they illuminate the path to prosperity in our long journey through life.

There are many social skills for us to acquire. Greeting each other appropriately is the simplest skill to learn, while knowing how to invade another's privacy without seeming to intrude is among the hardest.

When we are socially adept we use a variety of stratagems to achieve our goals. Sometimes we make people laugh, sometimes we rely on charm, or good looks, or suave speech. When we are skilled socially we can spot another person's flaws, and understand how to use them without seeming to exploit. Whatever stratagem we choose to apply, social skills are the magic wand that lets us pass through the lives of others without friction.

Social skills teach us to pick up subtle signals about a person's thoughts, or their intentions, or their anxiety or discomfort at our approach. They teach us the secret of finding and connecting successfully with the people we need to further our endeavors. Because the people around us may not be the ones who can help us the most.

Nor may the people we need have the social skills to make them outgoing and easy to approach. Which puts the onus on us to smooth the path of our introduction. Acquiring social skills is to learn the art of frictionless convergence, painless parting, and the making of acquaintances who will welcome our return, and in time ripen into friendships.

Have you ever tried playing bowls, or tennis? If not, then when you start you probably won't enjoy playing these games as much as you enjoy watching someone else play. But if you take lessons, and your coach is skillful and clever, he will first make you learn the basics of the game, then let you beat him, then make sure you enjoy your triumph to the full. And after you have laughed off his praise, a love of the game will begin to slip into your heart bit by bit. You will no longer see it as daunting, and your slight anxiety will be replaced by anticipation.

The same applies to learning social skills. We may be daunted at first by the size of the challenge that faces us. But a clever coach will teach us how to make an angry person laugh, or a sad person relax; how to bring up delicate subjects, and ignore fools; how to laugh in the face of detractors, and then break through their hostility and be accepted in their midst.

There are many social skills that we require. To perfect them, we need to watch those who are already masters, and analyze their actions and their thoughts. The effort in learning how to play the game of life is worthwhile, for it will allow us to get closer to potential friends, avoid losing contacts who may prove valuable, and withdraw gracefully from those who are unsuitable. We will avoid the waste and distraction of unnecessary disputes, of fruitless battles that are not worth fighting - even if we could win them - and save our mental energy for the battles that matter.

With social skills comes the ability to choose friends wisely, and bind them to us. And the ability to spot people who are unsuitable, and be cautious in our dealings with them, while hiding any antipathy we feel, and showing them respect - whether deserved or not. That way, we avoid making enemies. When we can draw close to good friends, and stay calm in the face of enemies, we can say that we have acquired a good level of social skill.

Social skills make the difference between a person who is accorded respect without having to demand it, who remains popular and well regarded on the one hand; and a person who is disrespected and denied his dues, simply because he antagonizes those around him.

Results of not acquiring social skills

A. Being deprived of friends

We may board the ship of life as part of a crowd, and spend our journey caught up in what's happening on deck; but when the waves hit, we quickly discover that we are alone. We find that no one cares about us or our welfare, and that escaping the ship will require us to jump into the middle of the ocean.

Living our lives without friends is like living on a deserted island. To avoid such isolation we must make the effort to find friends. Then we must cultivate those friendships, like the olive trees we water for many years before they fruit. If we do not make this investment, we find - too late - that we have only acquaintances.

We may not feel comfortable sharing our emotions, hopes, dreams and thoughts with other people. We may feel that it is intrusive, and resent our privacy being invaded. But there are two types of invaders; those who intrude for malicious ends, and those who take an interest because they care. If we find the latter to be intrusive, it indicates that we lack social skills, and maturity. Because jumping alone into the ocean, and living on a deserted island, are against our nature. We all need to share.

It is important to keep our relationships in perspective, and to know who we can safely confide in and who we cannot. As long as we choose our friends wisely, we will not become vulnerable by sharing our secrets.

Friends often swap secrets, safe in the knowledge that each person's secret is safe with the other.

B. Befriending inappropriate people

Friends are seeds we sow one day, then water repeatedly through our interactions. If our friendship is good, the seed becomes a productive tree, and the friendship will bear fruit. But if our friend turns out to be a thorn tree, and we water the friendship for many years, the thorn tree will grow and the thorns become stronger. The danger of being wounded by being near it then increases.

Finding out too late that a friend is an unsuitable person can destroy our faith in friendship, and undermine our ability to be open with our other friends. The shock of such a discovery is great, and the harm deep.

Many of us fail to examine our friends critically. There is nothing wrong in asking a loan from a friend who has just informed us about a large sum of money coming his way, and then returning the money once his friendship has been demonstrated. If we pretend to be in a crisis, and he nevertheless excuses himself, we know he does not care much for our welfare. That is dangerous, and a good thing to find out before we rely on him at a critical stage.

C. Failing to recognize others' intelligence

Some people bury hatred in their hearts and believe it is hidden. But the truth is that it is obvious, because many people - especially those who have reached middle age - can discern others' emotions easily. With experience comes greater emotional intelligence, which helps us perceive and cope with the hidden emotions of those around us. If we lack social skills we may wrongly assume that other people are stupid. This will create many obstacles that hinder our dealings with them.

Picture a domestic help who doesn't hesitate to do her duties, and more, but fails to smile at requests made by the children of the family. It is clear to me that that she is uncomfortable with non-routine orders. I call her into my office and ask her about a recent meeting at my mother's house, attended by the rest of domestic helps in the family. Does she know who, among those helps, likes and dislikes her?

She replies that she does.

I tell her that she is intelligent in being able to understand others' emotions, but that she is not the only person with such intelligence. I add that she is a valued worker, and it is appreciated that she carries out work outside her job description. Yet, she gives out signals that indicate a hatred of her work, and even the children have picked up on this. As a result, we as parents feel uncomfortable. If she could impress the children more with her willingness, they would surely reciprocate by being warm towards her.

After this meeting, her demeanor improves.

D. Extremism

A person equipped with good social skills can choose the best strategy to achieve their social objectives. Sometimes they will use a smile, other times courtesy, or a pretence at being angry. Whereas people who lack such skills either become aggressive or grow defensive. They adopt the belief that "people only understand the logic of force" or "all the good people are gone, only bad ones are left", because they themselves lack the capacity for fine social distinctions.

The truth is that they don't have the social skills to bring out the best in people. Becoming accustomed to assuming that everyone is bad, and therefore treating them badly, they become extreme in their dealings with people, and less tolerant.

Life, wealth, work, and attaining the status of being a decent human being are just some of the many battles awaiting us. When the threat of war is always present, the victor is the person who chooses their battles carefully. There are many trumpets calling us to fight, but retreating should always be our first choice, because most battles are not worth fighting. Opening fronts at random will weaken us in the overarching war of life; we must be discriminating about where and when to stand and fight. An extremist never removes his military uniform. He fights every battle and answers every trumpet call, but fails to win a single encounter because his strength is dissipated.

Far better is to avoid losing anyone's affection to a slip of the tongue or careless mistake. Social skills could show our extremist a safe line of retreat, and that being content with a "propaganda" war is often a better choice. They could also instill in him the wisdom and tolerance that wins people's love, and make it easy for him to ignore or overlook others' flaws.

An extremist needs to be aware of his faults, and gain insight into the reasons behind his severity. If he understood his own faults better, he would be less harsh on those of others. Learning to have compassion will teach him to be tolerant, because whoever is compassionate will understand and forgive people's faults.

Tolerance starts in our hearts. It dictates that when we see other people's flaws, we pardon them. Because pardon and forgiveness elevate us to the level of angels, while extremism reduces us to the level of animals, who fight over food or trivial matters.

When other people make mistakes, it gives us an opportunity to demonstrate our humanity. Because if no one transgressed against us, how could we show forgiveness, tolerance and compassion? Their transgressions are our ladders to better ethics, an opportunity to reassess ourselves and to improve where we fall short of the standards we aspire to.

We can either triumph over them by insisting on asserting our superiority, and grinding their faces into the dust; or by acting ethically, and with compassion. Some people are reluctant to pardon transgressors, preferring to humiliate those they hate when their mistakes present an opportunity. But we should remember that we are all mortal, and will all depart this world, and that the challenge inherent in showing clemency is an opportunity to improve ourselves and reach our personal goals.

If we focus our minds on the harm extremism causes, and we take it on board, when extremism rears its head in our own thoughts we will recognize it more easily and have a better chance of turning it aside. Then we will find the path to tolerance easier to follow.

E. Destructive effect of anger

Anger is a destructive emotion that damages our thought processes and leads us to take destructive actions. When we allow it to destabilize our emotions, other people will notice, and will avoid social connections with us. We need to practice the skill of explaining our feelings rationally rather than displaying our anger.

A man enters a shop to return an item. He starts telling the shopkeeper, "I'm upset, I feel frustrated about having to come back here despite my busy schedule. I have wasted money on expensive gas driving here, and I am annoyed…." The seller cuts him off and asks "What is your problem?" He replies, "I'm trying to express my feelings, which are more important than the problem with your goods. I don't know you personally, but you represent the company responsible for causing this inconvenience, so will you please just accept responsibility for the problems that are making me angry?" He then completes his complaint without being cut off by the shopkeeper, and the shopkeeper is more helpful, and more willing to try to satisfy him.

If we are angry with someone but we are forced to continue dealing with them, it is important to explain the reason for our anger. Otherwise they will notice it, but not understand that it is caused by their actions. It would then be natural for them to think that we are displaying irrational personal hostility, and to react in a negative way. This would only exacerbate the situation. But if we calmly explain why we are upset, they are more likely to understand and empathize with our problem.

FOUR: INTERNAL EQUILIBRIUM

UNDERSTAND INTERNAL EQUILIBRIUM

I was queuing at Frankfurt airport to recover sales tax before leaving the European Union. Ahead of me in the queue, a female customs officer was explaining to a woman from my country that in Germany, if the amount of tax is large, she must have her passport stamped as a precautionary measure before the monies can be refunded.

The woman couldn't understand what she was being told, or that this was a procedure unique to Germany. Seeing that the conversation was going in circles, I stepped in to try and help.

"Would you mind if I explained to my countrywoman why you cannot yet refund the money?"

The security officer said I was welcome to go ahead.

I therefore explained the situation to the female traveler, who duly left to get her passport stamped. I was then processed by the customs officer, who gave me a refund without telling me to get my passport stamped. Out of gratitude, and seeing that she was stressed, I offered her some kind words.

"Your job is difficult, and exhausting."

She agreed, nodding her head. "And I work twelve hours a day."

"That's too much!" I replied. "But you know, as exhausting as those long hours are, there is something even more exhausting you need to take notice of."

"What's that?" she asked.

"You are getting tired of people, psychologically. I noticed how much it affected you when you were trying to explain to the woman in front of me."

"I try hard to be sympathetic, explain the situation, and ask the passengers to proceed to their journey. But sometimes they just stubbornly refuse. It upsets me to see other passengers being delayed."

I asked if she wanted to hear a solution. She said that by all means, she would be pleased to listen.

"The root cause of your problem is that passengers don't always understand what your job is. So, if you forgave them their lack of understanding, you'd be less stressed."

"How can I forgive them, when some nationalities in particular just stubbornly refuse to listen?"

"Excuse their ignorance, and their lack of sophistication, and bear in mind that they are worried about losing their money; then you will feel more relaxed."

Understanding the influences that affect our thoughts often makes it easier to cope with day to day events, and makes adverse experiences less stressful. The customs officer thought her problems stemmed from the length of her working day, which was something beyond her control. She also thought that language and culture barriers were causing misunderstanding, and therefore conflict, between her and the passengers she dealt with. She saw these as being external influences, all of which were beyond her control.

But this analysis of her problems was faulty. She was actually suffering from two internal issues, both of which she could have dealt with. One was ignorance of the factors that were preventing her reaching internal equilibrium; and the second was concern about her own treatment of the passengers. Because she was young and inexperienced, she failed to recognize what was happening, and failed properly to analyze her own emotions.

Although she thought the passengers were simply being obstreperous and obstinate, they actually had legitimate grounds for concern. They thought that if they left the queue they were at risk of losing the chance to reclaim their tax. Money is precious to us all, and it was reasonable of them not to want to lose the substantial sums they were reclaiming.

It is true that the customs officer was patient with them and treated them well, but because she was hiding her real feelings this came at a high cost that left her feeling stressed. If she had managed to understand the passengers' concerns, she would have empathized with them, rather than feeling hostile or put upon. She might also have found better ways to persuade them, such as displaying an explanatory notice in their language. Instead, she ended up in a vicious circle of mental exhaustion, stress, and poor job satisfaction.

Our minds are filled with a swirl of thoughts and emotions that we often fail even to recognize, let alone know how to deal with. The case of the customs officer is just one example that illustrates the need to deal effectively with these currents of thought. It also shows that empathizing with others will benefit us too, by reducing the stress we suffer and restoring our internal equilibrium. To reach internal equilibrium, we must learn to understand our minds and to analyze our thoughts.

When do we reach internal equilibrium?

We achieve a state of inner peace when we feel positively towards both our past and the present, and are prepared to deal with whatever the future holds.

How to achieve internal equilibrium

Even without a beautiful face, a child's inner beauty still shines through. His features may not be classically proportioned, but his innocence is still apparent. We were all once innocent children. Strangers to envy and hatred, we knew only how to love. If we fought with our friends one day, the next we would wake up cleansed of our anger and ready to laugh and play with them once more. Our hearts were light, our emotions pure, and our intentions benign.

Internal equilibrium is when we recapture that essential goodness, but as adults. To achieve it, all we have to do is remove the obstacles that are holding us back from our natural state.

Obstacles to internal equilibrium

Internal equilibrium requires us to regain the innocence that we had at birth. This means examining our emotions, thoughts and motives to ensure that we always act in a way that promotes the five equilibriums we have discussed in this book. It also means adopting a positive attitude towards relationships and our inner thoughts.

The main obstacles preventing us from achieving internal equilibrium are:

1. Failing to focus on what is important

Being preoccupied with our surroundings distracts us from examining ourselves. When we were young our minds were at peace and we were far more accepting of life. Now that we have grown and want our estates to grow too, we pay too much attention to our material assets, and too little to good intentions and having a pure heart. Having failed to water the seeds of our childhood innocence, we have left it to wither and die, concentrating instead on our day to day affairs.

When we buy an expensive device and get home to find it doesn't work, do we stop to examine our feelings, or do we just plough on with getting it fixed as soon as possible? Examining our feelings concerning events is something we do too rarely. Instead, we let our anger rage, consumed as we are by the wasted time, money and inconvenience that having to return the device causes us. We are frustrated that we will have to travel all the way back to the showroom, spending money on transport or gas. We wonder why on earth we didn't check the goods before we left, given that the journey is so far? We also recall the bad customer service the showroom is reputed to offer, and that makes us anxious about how they will respond. Soon, we find ourselves wishing we had never bought it in the first place. We then remember someone advising us not to buy it, and that just annoys us more.

Often in life we put off things we consider to be less important, and we focus on the things we think are urgent. If our bank account is suddenly credited with an enormous sum, as likely as not we will ring the bank straight away to find out where it comes from. But what we fail to do in life is to look behind the immediate events, to try to understand our underlying thoughts, and why we prioritize matters in the way we do.

Ranking events by their importance is a fundamental attribute of our planning skills. But so too is understanding what influences our moods, and how we can control those influences. We ignore our mood because we think it is beyond our control. But in fact, it is not.

2. Ignorance

We know so little about the world. And although each new dawn heralds fresh discoveries, these discoveries don't expand our knowledge to any great degree, they just serve to highlight how much more there is yet to learn. In all that we undertake, we are bound by bonds of ignorance that restrict our actions, just as an insect is bound by the sticky silken strands of a spider's web.

The only way for an insect to escape is to break free of the cobweb, and the only way for us to expand our horizons and begin to understand the world is to break free of our bonds of ignorance. We are just as ignorant about ourselves as we are about the world; we don't even understand the workings of our own minds. Those minds act as scales that weigh issues before coming to a conclusion. But our ignorance is like an unstable link in the chain that supports the scales. Flexing this way and that way, it makes reaching balance impossible.

Recognizing what we do not know about our inner world is the first step towards achieving internal equilibrium. To be able to deal with our ignorance, we first need to be able to recognize it. The links that make up the chain are many, but among the most important are:

A. Ignorance of the decision-making centers

At the start of the twenty first century, doctors studying patients with head injuries discovered that the brain functions using different centers for different tasks. An injury in one center, for example, might make it impossible for a patient to speak, while an injury in another may make conceptualization difficult. By careful observation, and the use of scanning devices, they found that people use different parts of the brain to take different types of decisions, depending on the processes required. It is important to be aware of these different centers, because taking a decision using the wrong one may lead to a bad decision. In fact, using the wrong center to take a decision is one of the principal barriers to internal equilibrium.

Applying logic to take a decision leads to a balanced choice that meets both our long term and short term needs. Whereas taking a decision based purely on emotion will satisfy only our short term needs. It may bring us instant peace, but it does so at the expense of our long term interests.

If our rights are trampled on at work or in society we may avoid complaining, for fear of being labeled 'difficult,' or of provoking consequences that are far worse. Yet our long term interests demand that we do protect our rights by complaining.

The decision not to complain is one taken by our emotional center, whereas our logical center urges us to do exactly the opposite. Logic and emotion are like two advocates. Each addresses us in turn, and we listen and decide. Emotion speaks in a voice that is urgent and shrill, while logic's voice is soft and low; but it is the one we must listen to, as it serves our long term interests.

B. Ignorance of our minds' calculations

Changing something in our life takes time. The key to achieving such change is to understand the mental processes that determine how we choose between different courses of action. Although our minds work as predictably as calculators, unless we have sufficient self-awareness to understand how they operate, we cannot steer them towards the changes we want to achieve.

Perhaps we want to lose weight, and we focus our thoughts on how good it would be to look slimmer. First we think about it, then we start taking steps aimed at reducing our food intake. Then we find that we are failing to lose weight, so we try something different. That doesn't work either, and feeling that the whole idea is hopeless we relapse back into overeating, and remain obese.

The reason our good intentions failed is that we didn't understand the equations in our head that determined whether we would actually make a diet stick. If we have such a strong desire to eat that the pleasure it brings outweighs our logical acceptance of the need to diet, our diet will fail. If the value of food to our brain is greater than the value of leaving the food uneaten, we will eat it.

Similarly, if a man who wants to quit smoking places a higher value on the pleasure smoking brings than on his children, and family, and even his life, he will continue to smoke. He may be attracted conceptually to the idea of not smoking; but if his life without smoking would be worthless, what chance is there of him quitting?

Understanding the equations that govern our actions requires that we have self-awareness; that we monitor ourselves and analyze our internal thought processes. Our minds always choose the course of action that we perceive as offering the highest value; if that course of action is harmful we need to examine our motivations and find a way to re-prioritize, to change the values we assign to each option.

Another example is the man who hoards worthless possessions. No matter how much we try to persuade him, he will not throw junk away. He may wish he had a junk free house, but his emotional centers tell him the junk is valuable. As long as he perceives it as valuable he cannot bear to be parted from it. To change his behavior, we have to change his perception. Perhaps it would help to take him to the market and show him the worthlessness of the sort of junk he is clinging to. Repeated efforts to change the value he assigns to his junk are the best way to change his behavior.

The same applies to the person who swears repeatedly, or who bolts their food without chewing. Such habits can only be overcome if the person involved is able to reassign the values they place on their conduct. Simply criticizing them will not help. It may even make them more determined to cling to their uncouth ways. But make them see that it coarsens their image in others' eyes, and they may begin to change their assessment of the behavior's worth. If the inveterate swearer can be made to realize that, far from conveying a powerful message, swearing simply alienates the people listening, they may come to value swearing less highly. With that crucial step taken, they will understand the need to find better ways to convey their message.

C. Ignorance of the complexity of change

Wanting to change our lives is the first step, but achieving that change requires persistence. Simply setting goals to promote our equilibriums does not guarantee that they will be met, for the obstacles in our path are substantial and complex. To succeed, we need to have the insight that lets us understand these obstacles. And the tenacity to keep trying to overcome them.

D. Ignorance of mental processes

Some people discover themselves through insomnia, their minds becoming alert and wakeful when they try to sleep and condemning them to lie half the night with their thoughts racing. Such a pattern often becomes established to the point where it is very difficult to break, but the compensation for their lost sleep is a deeper degree of self-awareness.

Some people consider their eating habits, and find that their perception of food as a source of pleasure rather than nourishment, is the reason why they cannot lose weight. Even once this awareness has been gained they discover that changing the perception is not simple. They are then forced to admit how little they really understand about their own thought processes.

Other people are afflicted by obsessive compulsive disorder, and fall constant prey to their doubts and suspicions. Have they or haven't they switched off the gas, brushed their teeth, or done whatever other thing they cannot stop thinking about?

In each case, the conclusion is that we need greater insight into our own minds. These are just a few examples that show the extent of our ignorance about ourselves. There are many others that life offers, all of which make us stop, look at ourselves, and see strangers, as though we are spectators watching our own lives played out in a bubble of ignorance that we cannot penetrate.

Studying our inner thoughts may lead to a feeling of disassociation, as though there is some other being within us who controls our emotions, our mood and our impulses. Such a sensation is a strong argument for making the effort needed to learn about the workings of our inner mind.

Because there is so much to take in, we need to approach the exercise slowly, gradually expanding our knowledge and understanding. To some extent our path can be smoothed by reading what scholars have written about the process of analyzing our thoughts. This will take us part of the way along the path of understanding. But the rest of the path we have to navigate under our own steam, feeling our way forward step by step, until we reach the understanding we seek.

Whoever searches for equilibrium will find that self-awareness is essential. When problems arise in our lives, be they financial, social or physical, we may imagine that the cure is an external solution. Whereas in fact, our success in dealing with them will stem from the way we manage our internal thought processes, starting with the priority we assign to such problems. Are they really as important as we believe? Or would we do better to sideline them, and focus our energies on more important issues?

Choosing which issues to deal with is half the battle won. An insult that would cause a less wise person to lose their temper, and fight to the death to avenge, might best be ignored as a trivial issue. It can only harm us as much as we let it. With proper control of the internal workings of our mind, its impact can be avoided and we can continue our day in good spirits, saving us the wasted energy of dealing with it. Everything depends on the viewpoint we choose to adopt. If we tell ourselves that a man attacking us with his tongue is as bad as using his fists, and that our dignity is priceless, we will be trapped into fighting back. But if we tell ourselves that ignoring fools is always the wisest policy, we can calmly get on with our day.

The wiser we are, the better able we are to rationalize external threats, assess them calmly, and deal only with those that are genuinely harmful, thereby using our minds to nullify threats that other people would be damaged by.

To achieve and maintain internal equilibrium, we therefore need to gain self-awareness, and use it to navigate around the obstacles in our path. The most formidable of which is ignorance about, and lack of control over, our own mental processes.

E. Ignorance of Our state of mind

Our emotion is our state of mind. It may be satisfaction, anger, laughter, dismay, fear, or many others. Seeing our emotions for what they are, and understanding their effect on our lives and decisions, is the beginning of our journey to self-awareness and therefore to change.

We can begin the process of improving ourselves by asking whether a particular emotion is healthy or harmful to us? Will it promote peace of mind, or destabilize us? And would giving in to it spell disaster for our long term plans, or would it improve our future wellbeing?

Understanding our emotions begins with asking "What am I feeling right now? Why am I uncomfortable? Why am I angry?" Anyone who doesn't understand their inner world will find it difficult to control their reactions to events, or their state of mind. The first step to controlling our state of mind, is understanding it.

We should analyze the emotions that inform events as an integral part of analyzing those events. That means analyzing the motives behind our actions, and our reasons for behaving in a certain way. It may be counter intuitive, but understanding what is happening around us is often easier than understanding what is happening inside our own heads. Because what we don't know about the events, machines, and people around us can be learned from other sources; but when it comes to understanding our own motivations and thoughts we are utterly alone, stranded in a desert without signposts or guidance. If we cannot find our own way through the tangle of our thoughts, no one else can help us.

We should ask ourselves: why are we laughing? Is it because the situation is genuinely funny? Or is it because we are in the mood to laugh? For when someone has made us laugh once, the laughter becomes infectious, and that person gains the power to lighten our mood.

Or are we one of those people who laughs when we are in trouble, to mask our fear? Understanding the reason for our emotions makes us better at handling the present, and better prepared to face the future. If we feel anger we should search for its root cause. If we feel apprehensive, we should examine our thoughts to understand what it is that we are really afraid of. The same with all our negative emotions; we should delve into their underlying causes, rather than simply making shallow assumptions. We should note when these feelings visit us, identify causal relationships with specific people, places or events, and rationalize their appearing. That way, we can begin to understand them, aim to control them, and possibly even eliminate them.

Internal equilibrium environment

Containing our emotions

We are sometimes invaded by a whole stream of emotions simultaneously. Like a bundle of sticks, we could easily deal with one or two on their own, but not all of them together. The result is that we are overwhelmed.

Returning to our example in which we bring a device home from the showroom, only to find that it doesn't work, if we concentrate too much on the device's failure we will pay too little attention to what is happening inside our head. That would be a mistake, as it is important to our health that we analyze every emotion confronting us. If we find that we are angry, we must ask ourselves why. For example, "The reason I am annoyed is because I ignored the advice I was given, because I was too busy to consider it properly. And concerning my anger at the company's negligence, I must contact the manager and request compensation for my transport costs. Or ask him to deliver a replacement device to my home.

And if he asks why I didn't check the goods at the showroom, I will explain that the salesman wrapped it before I had a chance."

We must consider objections, and not be unsettled by them. "I accept it would not be normal to give compensation, so I am prepared for him to refuse. In which case, I will grow from this experience by making it a lesson for the rest of my life, never to give in to the beguiling assurances of salesmen, and always to check what I buy before leaving."

In this way will we benefit from our negative experiences, by learning lessons for the future, and by gaining deeper insight into our own minds. By addressing every negative emotion we feel, we can put our minds at ease, and turn a negative into a positive experience in which we regain control.

If someone treads on our toes, scuffing our new shoes and reigniting the pain in our injured foot, our emotions will be ones of anger and retaliation. But anger is incompatible with our ethics, our drive to be more tolerant, and our aspiration to pardon those who harm us.

At first, controlling this anger will be as difficult as preventing a volcano from spewing molten lava. But practice and persistence will increase our capacity for self-control, ultimately leading us to the point where we can give them our other shoe and ask they do justice between the two, thereby deflecting anger with humor. Then the transgressor will fall in love with our morals. He will know that we have the skill to transform situations, and an attitude of tolerance, that we love to pardon wrongs, and that we laugh and win people over. Is this not all better than spewing molten lava?

Our anger at having our foot trodden on is just one example of emotion interfering with our decisions. Life is full of similar examples, which in each case require us to search for our peaceful centers and ignore the lure of harmful and distracting emotions. To reach those peaceful centers we need to know what's going on inside us, and learn how to contain our emotions.

B. Factoring in our internal costs

A relative may offer us a ride to the airport at a lower fare than a taxi. This will suit us financially, but is it the best choice when looked at in the round? When we bear in mind the fact that he will very possibly turn up late, whereas we could hail a taxi easily from the street and therefore be sure of arriving on time, the 'cheaper' price looks less attractive.

If we are forced to wait for him we will become stressed, for fear of missing our plane; and the cost to our internal equilibrium of being stressed may well outweigh the reduced cost of the fare. We cannot assess the true price clearly, unless we see the equation through the lens of our internal equilibrium; and we cannot do that unless we have the self-awareness that makes it possible to judge how the different factors will affect our state of mind.

Putting pessimism in perspective

A healthy dose of pessimism is as indispensable as our morning cup of coffee. But like coffee, too much of it is harmful, and will ruin our sleep. Controlled pessimism should be used to rationalize our decisions, to keep our feet on the ground, and to help plan for all eventualities. But it is a powerful seasoning that if over used can dull our senses and open us to hopelessness.

We should learn to move our sense of pessimism from our emotional center to our logical center. Rather than allowing it to infuse us with a nonspecific and destructive worry about what the future holds, we should apply it logically to help us identify and prepare for future problems. We should learn to use it in tune with optimism, as a balance, and we should learn how to combine the two to help us see future scenarios more clearly. When applied in this way, pessimism helps us take sensible precautions against specific threats.

Some people are always pessimistic. For these people, life quickly loses its shine. Conversely, if we are over-optimistic and ignore possible dangers, we are setting ourselves up for a fall, and ultimately depression; because anticipating and being prepared for failure is the only way to succeed.

Therefore pessimism in the context of planning is prudent, while planning within a context of pessimism is a disaster. Life is very complex, and pessimism teaches us to foresee harmful possibilities and prepare for them. Such foresight is difficult for those simple minded souls who insist on keeping their brains clear of complex thoughts; who shut down their thoughts each day with a blank sheet, and open the next morning with an equally blank sheet.

Fighting negative thoughts

Negative thoughts can manifest themselves in many ways, such as telling ourselves we are a failure, or blaming our shortcomings on others, or adopting extreme perfectionism that stops us starting a task because we fear that we will not achieve the expected standard, or perhaps just severe depression.

Whichever manifestation we experience, they are all mental afflictions that see us spinning in an evil vortex from which we cannot escape. Reaching internal equilibrium is impossible for anyone in the grip of such negativity, because negativity is like a virus that inflames our emotional centers, vaporizing logical thought and replacing it with unstable emotions. Like worms eating away at the logical center of our brain, negative thoughts render us incapable of rational thought. The best weapon we have against them is awareness. Armed with such awareness, we can defeat them.

Our motives

Our motives are the hidden intentions behind our actions. They are part of the internal mechanics of our minds, the reasons that drive our behavior, the needs that move us, the secret desires we aim for, the ambitions we dream of. A motivation could be as simple as ordering a sandwich to calm our mid-morning hunger, or as complicated as the need to excel at a sport or in business to impress our peers, or send a message of excellence to a lover.

The reasons underlying our motives may be clearly apparent to us, or they may be deeply hidden. They may be conscious thoughts, or they may be impulses based on forgotten childhood dreams that revisit us and exert a powerful influence.

How little we know about our motives

Even psychologists may fail to understand their motivations, because true self-knowledge is difficult to achieve. We are driven by many impulses, some clear and others obscure, all layered on top of each other in a complex pattern.

Sometimes we are driven by a need to achieve clear and present goals. Other times, the impulses driving us are buried deep in our past. They could be childhood rivalries that survive into adulthood, spurring us to outperform siblings, acquaintances or friends. There is nothing wrong with such rivalry, provided it manifests itself as a positive force that spurs us on, rather than a malicious force that wishes another person harm. Such malice is like a contagion that infests our hearts and darkens them. It should be cleaned by praying for those we envy, and remembering that we each have blessings in one form or another. Otherwise it grows, and breeds jealousy, hatred, and a desire for revenge. When these emotions become the driving force of our actions, we descend into a dark and bitter world.

Buy a ticket to your internal world

Acknowledging our ignorance is the first step towards understanding ourselves; and admitting that we have a lot to learn about ourselves is the key that unlocks access to our internal world. Because when we think we know ourselves well, and reject the possibility that we may be ignorant about our internal world, we fail to delve deeply into our thoughts. And failing to delve deeply prevents us from tasting the pure waters that lie hidden in our depths.

Such self-exploration is essential to true self-understanding. Because examining our motivations and emotions, and the reasons underlying them, requires us to deconstruct our minds and rebuild them, in order to gain true insight. We will only go through this difficult process if we admit our ignorance; why strive for understanding, unless we accept that there is knowledge we have yet to gain?

What are our hidden motives?

It is easy to accept that we cannot cook, or that we cannot fly a plane. But it is less easy to accept that we are unable to understand our own motivations.

A man walks up to two people sitting at a dining table and insults them. They respond angrily to his insult, and he apologizes. After the apology, the first person at the table forgives him, while the second continues to remonstrate angrily. In fact his offense is intensified by the apology, because he regrets his angry response, believing it has made him look foolish and hasty. And his irritation is increased by the fact that the other person apologized, which makes his own anger stand out as ungracious. By apologizing so quickly, the man has denied him the chance to look magnanimous.

Understanding the mechanics of the situation requires that we understand the motivations of each of the actors. The first person at the table has done well; he is pleased at having received an apology, despite the fact that he took his revenge by returning the insult. He has extracted everything he can from the situation, and if he reflects on what has happened he will realize that he has gained more than he deserves.

The second person at the table is not pleased, because he wanted to be the one who initiated the apology. Instead, his continued anger made him look unreasonable, when he wanted to look gracious. But if he reflects on the situation, he will realize that he should have expected the man who threw the first insult to apologize quickly, since to sustain the insults for long would have been extremely aggressive. Therefore he has no one but himself to blame for losing his chance to look magnanimous.

Dealing with our motives

Determining what we don't know about people's motives is our first goal. Actually finding out enough to understand those motives is then a challenge, but it is one that is worth the effort. Over time, as we observe and learn, understanding people's motives becomes easier. But we need to disassociate ourselves from our own emotions, to be dispassionate, or we will see things through our own eyes rather than the eyes of the people we are watching. Only by distancing ourselves from our emotions can we reverse the process, and learn about ourselves, and our motives, from the behavior of those we observe. In the course of which we will hopefully learn to recognize our own character flaws, and to overcome the false impression that we are different from - and better than - the people we are studying. By seeing their faults we will understand our own, shedding light on the dark recesses of our mind that previously we had feared to enter.

This is a valuable step, for it brings us closer to the self-knowledge that is the font of internal equilibrium. Once we achieve a level of self-knowledge we will find that we are more relaxed and more fulfilled, and it will encourage us to keep exploring our inner recesses to find out more.

There are always things for us to learn about ourselves, be they good or bad. Armed with our new self-knowledge we can unravel many of our internal issues. Perhaps we have long been irritated by the presence of our younger brothers, but never examined why. We have been condescending towards them, or we have treated them badly, but only now can we admit that the root of this behavior is our jealousy at their better house, job, degree, intelligence, or other success. Discovering the truth about our failings may make us look ugly in our own eyes, but it will also allow us to return to equilibrium. And the truth is that most of us have such jealousy, but fail to admit it.

Understanding our motivations will help us improve

Once we begin to understand our internal motivations, we can gain better insight into our emotions. We can then start to tame our consciousness, to anticipate its convoluted ways and to gain some control over it, rather than being ruled by it blindly.

As we have seen before, there are those who swear habitually. Perhaps they began in their youth, when they believed that such words made them look mature and confident. Now, even though they may want to stop swearing, they are conditioned by years of habit. Once they realize why they swear, and gain the self-knowledge that lets them understand their thought processes, they are better able to fight the habit, and master it, rather than being its victim. They come to see that these words are damaging to their image, and they realize that they need to change. With that crucial conviction gained the balance within their mind changes, and the habit they could not break becomes breakable. Such is the power of self-knowledge, because understanding motives is the key to gaining control of our mind.

Developing an irrational prejudice against people we meet is not unusual. They have done us no harm, and we have no idea why we dislike them. Yet we feel uncomfortable in their presence. Only by asking ourselves why we dislike them, and delving deeper into the inner workings of our minds, can we begin to understand our inner psyche. Our prejudice may be based on something very minor – the way a person moves their hands when they speak, or the way they invade our personal space by standing just a little too close when they are speaking. We may not even be able to identify this much reason. The source of our dislike may be buried too deep for us to fathom. Perhaps on a subconscious level they trigger some childhood memory of a person we disliked, or of a situation that hurt us. Or there is a point of similarity between this person and someone we once knew and hated. The current dislike is then like a fossilized impression of a long past situation, whose outline lingers in our minds long after the real memory has faded.

To understand any of this we must have a degree of self-awareness about our emotions. It is not the solution to this specific dislike that matters; it is the principle underlying it that we need to find. The particular person in front of us will soon leave, but the problem they have thrown up in our thoughts must still be analyzed and answered if we are to progress in our self-understanding. Otherwise the opportunity they have offered us will be wasted.

We should remember two things:

Firstly, that we do not need to harbor hostility to people we dislike, even if they deserve it. Treating them well is beneficial to us as much as them, because it strengthens our moral character.

Secondly, that good motives benefit us too, by helping us to reach spiritual equilibrium. We may fail in business because we fall ill and cannot attend to our company; or we may fail to give charity because we have too little to live on ourselves. But there is no excuse for failing to have good intentions. They cost nothing and are freely available if we choose to adopt them. So why not avail ourselves of this free opportunity to do good and strengthen ourselves?

Our thoughts and beliefs

Our thoughts and beliefs are integral to the workings of our inner mind. Yet they can lead us astray. At the beginning of this book we discussed the concept of happiness, and found that everlasting happiness does not exist. Yet we found also that many people believe in it, and seek it; even going so far as to make this non-existent illusion the focus of all their energy, and a guide to all their actions. This conviction that everlasting happiness exists is a dangerous mistake. "Dangerous" because it distorts our perception of reality.

We should question the accuracy of our beliefs, demanding proof to justify them and asking ourselves how they benefit us. We will then find that some bring us no benefit at all. It is for this reason, and because our thoughts and beliefs have a special role to play in helping us reach equilibrium, that I allocated a chapter on managing equilibrium to address them.

Wrong timing

If we live in a city with high summer temperatures, we will discover in time that an air-conditioner's efficiency depends on it being topped up with refrigerant gas. If the weather is hot and humid and the gas is not topped up, ice can form on the compressor, reducing the unit's performance. Being aware of this simple fact will prevent us from sweltering in the summer heat when the issue occurs, because all we need to do is switch off the air-conditioner to let the ice melt, then switch it back on again. Meanwhile, we should top up the gas. If we ignore this, and respond to the rising temperature in the house by turning down the temperature control - in a futile attempt to force the machine to work harder and cool us down - we risk an expensive repair when the ice builds up to such an extent that the unit crashes. So the choice is to spend a little time and money on filling it with gas, or spend a lot of time and money replacing the compressor, plus three days suffering without air-conditioning while we wait for the technician to arrive.

The example of the air-conditioner is very similar to what happens in our minds when we experience anger and frustration. We don't need to know the mechanics of how our brain copes with anger; it is enough to know that when we are under pressure, piling more pressure on top by constantly analyzing our problems will make us worse rather than better, and eventually risks overloading our mind. We then reach a stage where our logical processes are overwhelmed by emotion. In effect, the emotional centers of our brain have taken over, and declared martial law, forcing our logical centers to retreat into silence.

When we are accused of making a mistake, or doing something wrong, regardless of whether the accusation is justified, we need to stay calm and rational rather than reacting with excessive emotion. When we learn to value getting to the truth of the matter, and expanding our understanding, more than we value imposing our view on others, or protesting, we take the first step on the long journey towards self-control and inner equilibrium.

If we have a dispute with a friend over an issue, and he has previously offended us over other matters, it is difficult to think clearly and impartially about the current dispute. Even if we are in the wrong, and we deserve everything he has said to us, it is unlikely that we will see it.

Dale Carnegie in "*How to Win Friends And Influence People*" recounts that he always used to delay responding to insulting messages for two weeks, to let his temper cool before replying. We need to distance ourselves from a problem to see it clearly. When we allow ourselves to become hot and bothered as a response to stressful situations, we are turning down the temperature control of our air-conditioner at a time when it is already struggling to cope. The wise person instead makes a conscious effort to relax, to slow their mental tempo, dissolve those ice crystals and cool their anger before it shuts off their rational thought and replaces it with turgid emotion.

Understanding events accurately requires a cool head and impartial judgment. It also requires self-analysis, awareness of our thought processes, and keeping a careful eye on how we react to events that touch us deeply.

Failing to make use of other equilibriums

When our internal equilibrium is upset there are several ways it can be restored. Sometimes it can be helped by our spiritual equilibrium, other times by our social equilibrium or financial equilibrium.

Sadness is an inevitable part of life. But the stress it causes us can in part be alleviated by seeking out a friend to share our pain, and in return receiving comforting attention. Sometimes we can reduce our stress by spending money. Gifts are cheap and they can make the people around you friends for life. Whereas quarreling with a salesman over a small amount is far more trouble than it is worth. The stress it engenders and the mental energy you waste cannot be justified by any trifling saving you make.

As a youth I used to relate my day's events to my father, who then dispensed sound advice. He once displayed astonishing wisdom by saying, "My son, a problem that can be fixed by money is a trivial problem. Since it has an easy solution, don't hesitate to solve it." Many "problems" exist only in our heads, because we are reluctant to spend even a small sum to solve them. There is nothing wrong with solving problems with money, if we have it. It is far more foolish to let small matters bother us disproportionately, when we have an easy means of solving them. Our objective in life is to achieve our goals, not to impede others in achieving theirs.

Making use of other equilibriums can help us overcome even the most severe internal dilemma. Drawing on our relationships with our loved ones is a valuable way of cooling our mind when it's wilting beneath the oppressive heat of calamity. And spiritual equilibrium makes it more bearable to cope with the loss a loved one, because it tells us we shall meet them again one day. While physical equilibrium, promoted by exercise and walking, will fill our free time and help us cope with temporary loneliness.

Internal morbidity

Sometimes we suffer mental illnesses such as severe depression, where we are upset with everything around us, cry constantly, and feel that the world is a dark place full of despair. In such cases this book will be of no use, because we cannot then restore our equilibrium on our own, and we need specialist help.

Our mental health is like our physical health. When we are healthy we do not need to ask a doctor how to eat, or how much we should eat. But when our bodies become ill we need a doctor to advise on all aspects of our care.

This book does not claim to address every single obstacle preventing us reaching internal equilibrium, for they are too many to mention. It is enough to be aware of the principle that we must constantly monitor our internal equilibrium, and if it requires specialist help, we must seek it.

FIVE: SPIRITUAL EQUILIBRIUM

What is the spirit? Our spirit is the invisible glue that enables us to function as a conscious being and gives us the ability to make choices in life. Although we cannot know the detailed nature of the spirit, this ignorance should not prevent us believing in its existence, and benefiting from it.

What benefits does our spirit bring?

At some point in our lives we all experience negative events that are out of our control. Being aware of and able to recognize our spiritual dimension helps us to cope with these events, and to make sense of them. Our spiritual dimension also helps us understand that events in our lives are not random and meaningless, but happen for a reason. To attempt to discover this purpose is a worthwhile challenge, in which we play the role of a student taking a masterclass in the workings of the universe.

Without a spiritual dimension to guide us, we would not take notice of the messages, advice and teachings of the Lord of the Universe. The spirit is therefore a beneficial and welcome concept to believe in, which helps us see the logical connections that only come together when we believe in God.

All theistic religions share the same basic concepts, in that they give us readily understood answers to the major questions that life poses.

109

Monotheistic religions explain our existence by telling us that God created the universe, whereas science tells us that the universe created us. Meanwhile, scientists are still working on trying to answer the question of "Who created the universe?" They may come up with a plausible explanation one day, but it is equally possible that the question will defeat them. If the answer comes after we have died, it will not help us much, as by that time it will be too late for us to change course and believe in God.

The issue of spiritual equilibrium is a valuable illustration of the benefits that come from believing in God. We live lives full of defects and constrained by many limitations. But religion tells us that life is simply a test, and if we pass that test we move to a plane where all limitations and barriers are removed. We then live a life full of happiness, where we can spend our time doing what we most enjoy.

Revisiting our earlier debate on happiness, this idea of life being a test offers a neat explanation of why we cannot achieve everlasting happiness in this life; if we could, what motivation would there be for passing the test? We endure hardships in this life, knowing that if we live righteously we will pass the test and receive our reward in heaven, thereby enjoying a future without the limitations and misery that constrain us now.

What is faith?

Faith is believing and having trust in God, and believing that the panorama of our lives is limited due to our limited perception. If we were omniscient, we would see far further and more clearly than our limited brains can now. But religion holds that God does not want our eyes to see further, as it would negate the need for faith. Only if his existence is uncertain, can we demonstrate our faith by believing in him.

To picture the world as it is, we must therefore imagine our own field of perception as a tiny sliver within a vast universe dominated by an eternal and omnipotent God. This limited field of vision is sufficient for our limited lifespan, and the limited understanding of our brains.

Our need to show gratitude

Showing gratitude to God by worshiping and thanking him is a basic need for every human. Its positive effect on our welfare is far reaching. In 2011, researchers carried out a study involving 219 participants[6], some of whom were asked to write daily letters of appreciation and gratitude over the course of three weeks, and some were not. At the end of the period the researchers found that those who wrote letters of gratitude had improved feelings of happiness and life satisfaction, and reduced depression, compared with those who did not write letters.

This study proves that when we express gratitude, we are benefitting ourselves rather than the person to whom we are expressing the gratitude. Showing appreciation and expressing gratitude make us feel more satisfied. The same applies to religion, which is all about showing our appreciation and gratitude to the one who deserves gratitude for creating us.

---

[6] J Happiness Stud (2012) 13:187–201

The Qur'an contains a saying that is relevant here; "We showed him the Way: whether he be grateful or ungrateful (rests on his will)." The meaning is that it is our choice whether we show gratitude for all that God has done for us, or we show ingratitude and skepticism; but if we do not show gratitude, we ourselves lose out, because our lives will be less balanced and less fulfilled.

Dangers insurance companies won't cover

Faith is the ultimate insurance against the harm that life throws at us. It insures us against sickness, poverty, old age, accidents and random events. When we get to know God we obtain comprehensive insurance against all risks, with the premium being paid whenever we demonstrate our faith through concrete actions. Once we accept God, we can be confident that we will be amply compensated for our faith; for he is the ultimate insurer, who does not take from us without giving back. His insurance keeps our lives in equilibrium, for it is a benefit of substance that can outweigh any loss we suffer.

Lighting the dark days

Our lives cannot reach equilibrium unless we believe the universe has a ruler. This is because no one's life is eternally pleasurable, and we must inevitably suffer losses that cause us deep pain. Loved ones die, the things we work for are denied us, the things we build are destroyed. We have to find ways to cope with these losses without our lives becoming empty and devoid of meaning. Otherwise we feel hopeless, living a bleak existence that leads to depression and suicide.

If we remember that God is going to compensate us for our suffering, we can overcome any misfortune. When we lose a son who is precious to us, and we are swept away by grief, our balance is restored when we realize that God will bring us back together one day. For faith tells us that there will be life after death.

This is why the spiritual dimension of our lives is the most important, and attaining spiritual equilibrium is the most important of all the equilibriums. One day we will die, and our other equilibriums will fade into oblivion. Our wealth, our honors, everything we value in life is a temporary benefit that will cease to matter. It is only our spirit that will endure.

Having faith restores us to equilibrium, because it reassures us that the misfortunes we are suffering in this life are only temporary. It also helps us accept the misfortunes that God sends; for although we cannot understand why he sends them, faith tells us that he acts for the greater good. What God wants for us may be different from what we want; but his actions are based on a greater understanding than ours.

Struggling against our fate

A woman less than fifty years old was struck by cancer, and became very depressed. She embarked on a course of treatment, and after six months of bitter struggle she was cured. Many years later the cancer returned. She became apathetic and resigned, complaining that God had inflicted the disease on her twice. "Why me?" she asked. She was angry and

113

upset, and resented her condition. Even though she had survived the first time, she was unprepared mentally to face the illness again. Rather than fighting the cancer, she spent her energy fighting what she saw as an unfair fate that was stealing her life away. She died, her last words being a complaint against God.

But no one is immortal, and she was wrong to expect to live for eternity without ever suffering a disease. Death comes to us all, and when it does it is easier to accept if we believe that we are going to meet God. Life is a test, and we have a choice as to how we approach it. If we have faith in God's existence, and we accept his word, we will accept that if we pass the test we will be brought into his presence. The other option is to fail the test, to reject God's word, and, like the woman in the story, to struggle against a harsh fate that offers no hope of salvation when we die.

If we pray to God, He may answer our prayers, heal our sickness and extend our life. But even if He does not, believing in Him, and praying to Him, will restore our spiritual equilibrium. It will make us feel more secure by reminding us that God is there, protecting us and looking after our interests, and by instilling in us a desire to meet God that will take away our fear of death. Rather than fighting against death, which is a battle we cannot win, we can accept the pain and exhaustion of any illness if we know that at its end we will meet God, and be happy and fulfilled in His presence.

Accepting our ignorance of God's purpose

When we have a headache, we look for its cause. If we do not find the cause quickly, we may take a pain killer to give us time in which to keep searching. We therefore tolerate our ignorance of the cause, until we are able to learn the truth.

Religion is the same. We do not always know why God approves or disapproves of certain actions. We do not know why He does not intervene in horrific events such as World War Two, the Holocaust, natural disasters, or other mass calamities. But if these terrible events cause us to lose our faith, it is like cutting off our head when we have a headache whose cause we cannot explain.

Rather than losing our faith, we should accept our ignorance of God's purpose.

How religion works to benefit us

It takes a positive act of will to have faith in God, and to believe that He is the owner of the universe and everything in it. But once we have made this decision it brings fulfillment to our lives, gives them meaning, and makes adverse events more bearable. It also changes our outlook on life, affecting us deeply in both our minds and our hearts. As time passes it becomes obvious who does and does not believe in God, because life is one long test to see who is fit for heaven.

Attaining spiritual equilibrium is a major challenge, but following God's guidance brings it within our reach. He gives us a head start by teaching us to believe that He is the Creator of the universe, thus providing a solid foundation on which we can build. If we then learn to trust in what we believe, we will act as a force for good in the world, and our good deeds will raise us to heaven.

Those who believe in God are able to find and concentrate on the positive aspects of harmful events. This makes their lives meaningful, less stressful, and helps them maintain a positive frame of mind. Non-believers, on the other hand, are like passengers being carried on a bus over which they have no control. Their beliefs are informed solely by science, which tells them that the bus is controlled by physics, chemistry, and the principles of engineering; while their view through the window is of trees, people and houses, all of which have been broken down into rational, mechanical concepts, leaving no room for God. Nor do they wonder about the direction the bus is taking, because that too is scientifically controlled.

Trusting in science leaves non-believers no scope for thinking about life's destination, because everything is controlled by scientific rules. Non-believers refuse to accept the existence of God, because they do not understand why any benign force would allow hunger, disease or earthquakes. Such tragedies, they say, can only be the actions of a cold, mechanical world, and their existence 'proves' that God does not exist.

But this error is a product of their taking a wrong approach. They do not understand the wisdom behind God's actions; and nor do they have the right to demand such an explanation. We are just creatures of God's creation, not gods ourselves. Why should we have the right to demand perfect knowledge of the universe He created?

A word for non-believers' ears

Some non-believers point to natural disasters as a way of justifying their lack of faith in God. But we should remember that many aspects of our own bodies are still a mystery to science, so how can we hope to understand the complexities of the wider universe? Demanding that God explains to us, His creations, the reasons for His actions, is like demanding that a king explains his decisions to his servants.

Let's imagine that we clone a rat, then move it from its cage at one end of the lab, to a cage at the other end. Are we expected then to explain to the rat all about its nutrition, and why we have moved it? And if we cause a disturbance in the lab when we clean it, must we then explain that too to the rat? How, then, can we expect God, who created us, to issue a detailed statement on earthquakes, volcanoes, movement of comets, and the reasons behind sickness and disease? My suggestion to non-believers is: talk to God personally, and forget what God does in others' lives. Focus on yourself, and your relationship with God, and you will certainly come to see God's goodness before long.

Understanding the nature of the relationship between humanity and God is essential to a proper understanding of how we should approach Him. He is our Creator, and we His creatures. He created the universe, and He created angels to pray to Him. But unlike these angels, we must choose whether to pray to God or not. We are free either to accept or reject God, to pray to Him or ignore Him. This choice is an important test of our faith. If we believe in God then we accept that we are His servants, and that our proper role is to worship Him. The more we worship Him, the better our grade in our test, and the more love He returns to us.

If we take this route, we accept that our relationship is one based on ownership, not mutual obligation. A servant has no right to demand favors from his master. Anything we ask of God is therefore sought by His grace, a merciful concession granted to us in return for our pleading. Understanding this relationship, and the test that it implies, is central to our mission. It is also the key to explaining events in our life, both large and small.

When we reach this understanding, we can truly call ourselves thinking creatures. The example of A rat is inaccurate because a rat does not think conceptually as we do, but it is a link to the idea of ownership rather than choice. Understanding that we are being tested in life requires us to know why we are being tested, and how God came to choose us.

The difference between a believer and a non-believer is that believers see dying as the start of a new journey, rather than the end of everything.

They have faith that after dying they will be transported to a new world, very much like the one they have just left, except that their destination will depend on the choices they made in life. If they chose wisely, their new world will be a happy place that reflects those choices. This belief profoundly affects the way believers act, for they understand that in their first life they are simply being tested.

Many people enjoy fulfilling lives, surrounded by beauty, and all the pleasures that life can bring; a loving spouse, rewarding children, friendly neighbors, a house planted with fruit trees and greenery that makes their existence as idyllic as the scenes depicted in a mosaic or a painting. Every aspect is perfect, vibrant, and rich. But without spiritual equilibrium these joys are transient, and end when we die. For spiritual equilibrium is the essential glue that holds our soul together, even after we depart this world. Without it, our pleasures have no long term meaning, and they will scatter from our soul just as a mosaic ultimately disintegrates into a jumble of colored stones.

The goal of spiritual equilibrium

If we use our lives to raise ourselves spiritually, step by step to a higher plane, the day will come when the prospect of dying does not terrify us. When that happens, we will have reached the point at which all our equilibriums are in balance, and we will have mastered one of the most difficult of all concepts to accept - that we are mortal, and our earthly vanities are transient. Having pushed them to the periphery of our thoughts, we can then focus instead on thinking about eternity. By this stage we will be fully confident that death is just the end of our test, the deadline for submitting our exam paper. And that the period after our death is only an interval during which others submit their papers, before the distribution of certificates can begin.

Having reached this high point in our existence, we can look back on everything we have done. Although it is a challenging target, our commitment will bring it closer. And with God's grace and guidance we will walk in the right direction, our hearts will be light, our mood tranquil, and emotions such as fear and anxiety will be banished by the act of finally reaching a state of equilibrium.

To reach our goal requires us to make a significant daily investment of time and energy, rising step by step, until the day arrives that we are told death is near; and we rejoice to meet the one we have longed to meet.

How to reach spiritual equilibrium

Although our bodies perish when we die, our souls remain. If we want our soul to achieve spiritual equilibrium, we must first recognize the reason for our creation: which was to worship. Worshiping our Creator, showing Him gratitude and appreciation, are needs planted deep inside us. Once we understand that we were created to worship, and we allow our lives to be guided by this knowledge, we start moving towards spiritual equilibrium. We then experience tranquility and satisfaction.

The solution to the problems inherent in reaching spiritual equilibrium comes from God, whose attributes overcome the restrictions of our bondage. He is "the powerful,' who mends our weakness; He is "the healer," who cures our sickness; He is "the honorable", who raises us up from our lowly state; and He is "the permanent", who cures us of our vanity and compensates for our mortality. Only through these attributes of God's can we reach spiritual equilibrium.

Attaining spiritual equilibrium requires us to be aware that God is watching us at all times. Acknowledging this is not easy, because if we acknowledge His constant presence we also need to take account of His wishes, recognize that He is testing us, and anticipate what actions He would approve of us taking.

People who place an emphasis on being materialistic never see this spiritual aspect of our lives, so they fail deal with it.

Since God is always present, and we are constantly being tested, we should ask ourselves what God would like us to do in any given situation. How would He want us to behave towards our spouse (the answer obviously being to show love and faithfulness) our children (to care for their needs and nurture them) our work life (to be honest and ethical) and so on...

When we approach someone to speak to them, we must remember that God is listening and ensure the truthfulness of what we say. When we sell goods, God is monitoring the honesty of our transaction. Equilibrium occurs when we act not only in our own interests, but also with regard to what will make God pleased with our conduct.

Obstacles to spiritual equilibrium

When someone discovers that their life is out of control, and that a fundamental imbalance has arisen, the cure is to remove the obstacles that are preventing them from re-connecting with God. Connecting with God should be a natural and easy process; if it is not happening, something must be obstructing it. Once these obstacles have been identified and removed, we will naturally gravitate back towards spiritual equilibrium.

Common obstacles to spiritual equilibrium include:

1. Intermediaries

Intermediaries are obstacles to reaching spiritual equilibrium. It is an appealing idea for some people to imagine that God appoints intermediaries to come between us and him. They find it comforting to turn to a human being and seek advice or reassurance about the best way to reach God. Perhaps they lack confidence in themselves, or in their worth, and believe that God will not hear them unless someone intercedes on their behalf. Such intermediaries may be scholars, religious individuals, or priests. Or they may simply be frauds and confidence tricksters, who profit from preying on their victim's fears and doubts.

No matter who they are, we do not need such intermediaries to approach God on our behalf. The ability to reach Him is innate in all of us. All we need to do is open our minds and our hearts, and He will hear us. The line of communication with God is clear and unobstructed; since there are no obstacles for us to overcome, no rivers for us to cross, we do not need bridges to aid us or facilitators to smooth our path.

God doesn't even need us to speak to know what we are saying; he simply looks into our hearts. Many mutes find God, and communicate with Him effectively. When we form words in prayer, these words are not for His benefit but for ours.

When we want to learn about religion, we should stick to facts and ignore opinions. We should also ignore 'information' about religion that cannot be shown to be authentic. We should follow religious scholars only insofar as their teaching leads us in a direction that pleases God. We should not follow anyone blindly, as this is a hindrance to our progress towards spiritual equilibrium. Our intelligence and our senses are the best guides as to what pleases God, which is why He did not instruct us to seek intermediaries. Instead, God has given us minds, just as it was God who gave their minds to religious scholars. Theirs are not necessarily better than ours. In fact, the most virtuous people are often unassuming and unrecognized, rather than those who are merely famous.

2. Activating religion

When we were young we often failed to notice important things. If we wanted something from our father, we would fail to gauge his mood before asking. As a result, we were disappointed when he refused. As we grew older we became more aware of the many considerations that needed taking into account, and learned to judge the mood and circumstances of those we were dealing with.

The same applies to life in general. As we grow up we learn to take account of traffic when crossing the road, and to judge our friends' characters to avoid those who were bad. We begin to appreciate the reasons why we become ill, and how to avoid accidents by taking proper care.

All these considerations add to our store of knowledge, and we mark them mentally with warning signs that prevent us repeating harmful mistakes. The most successful people are those who manage this process the best, allowing them to negotiate the hazards life throws in their path while those around them succumb.

In a similar vein, we also need to make warning signs for religion, to prevent us violating its laws. Some people choose to ignore religious prohibitions. They may perhaps justify this as being due to their life circumstances, or one of any number of other reasons; but most often it is simply that they are not honest, or they lack faith.

3. The theory of ever narrowing circles of faith

A theory that has been passed down through the ages holds that the good deeds and acts of worship that bring us closer to God radiate like concentric circles around Him. The more good acts we perform, the further we penetrate into the pattern, and the closer we draw to God. Yet there is always room to get closer still, by fulfilling more of His commands.

On the other hand there are those who make no effort to draw close to Him. They wrongly assume that religious observance is absolute, and since they cannot or will not keep the entirety of God's laws, they think it would be pointless or even hypocritical to keep any.

But this view is mistaken. There is no one who manages to keep every law. We all commit sins, we all fail to observe laws we should observe, we all fall short of perfection. Yet we are not all thereby cast out of God's presence. Religion is not absolute; God is forgiving and merciful towards sinners.

By keeping as many laws as we can, we improve our position. And the more we keep, the more the improvement. At the very least we can enter the first circle, the one furthest from Him, where anyone with the smallest element of faith in their hearts is admitted. If we are truly pious, and our hearts are full of faith and good acts, we can hope to enter the circle nearest to God.

Religion is a journey. We start it by dusting ourselves down to remove the remnants of the clay we were created from. We end it by raising our soul back to its Creator. There are many steps in between, as we slowly ascend the stairway towards God. Faith is a gradual process, with many gradations along the way. Some believe in God, but their belief is clouded by doubt. Whereas others are so unshakable in their belief that even dire misfortune cannot dissuade them.

I published an article entitled *Tuscany* in the *Qabas Kuwaiti* newspaper, in which I related coming across a Tunisian in Italy who gave drinking alcohol as an excuse for not performing daily prayers. "Don't give excuses about why you cannot perform daily prayers," I cautioned. "You can lay your prayer mat whenever it's time to pray, and keep praying until it cures you of the need to drink."

4. Refraining from God's words

Spiritual equilibrium begins with believing in the afterlife. When we cease viewing death as a catastrophe, we enjoy a more tranquil life and we take less harm from the shocks it throws at us.

Believing in the afterlife can only be achieved if we read God's words. This process also takes our minds off our daily cares, putting them into a broader context. The person who reads God's words on a regular basis builds a steadily growing trust in God, and moves the mountain of doubt, stone by stone with each word he reads, progressing steadily from a land of disbelief to a land of faith.

My father – may God be merciful with him- spent his lifetime chanting God's words, and looked forward to meeting Him. If, as a child, I wanted to speak to him, I had to wait until he had reached the end of a chapter. Breaking into my father's conversation with God was not allowed, as it was disrespectful. He became extremely animated during his prayers, rejoicing at the uplifting verses and despairing at those filled with anguish. He sometimes stopped to share a choice phrase that delighted him, amazed at the familiar tone of God's words, his eyes lighting up with happiness as though they were addressed to him personally.

One day, when he had become very sick, I tried to discuss an operation that might cure him. But he replied "My son, why are you afraid on my behalf? There is nothing more than death." He viewed death not as a disaster, but as an opportunity to meet God. He saw himself standing outside God's gates, and longed to enter and meet Him..

5. Ignorance

Ignorance obstructs our path to spiritual equilibrium. It comes in two forms:

A. Misapprehension of our true worth

An inflated belief in our own importance misleads us into thinking that it is unnecessary to worship God, and therefore becomes an important obstacle preventing our achieving spiritual equilibrium. If we imagine that we are equal to God, we will surely not worship Him.

Understanding our own insignificance brings our relationship with God back into a proper perspective. We exist to serve God; while He is our master. Understanding the nature of this relationship requires that we come to terms with our weakness and limited intellect.

We are small, puny creatures even in comparison with our own planet, the Earth. When we compare ourselves to the entire universe, our insignificance is magnified many times over. Our strength is infinitesimal compared to the power of the universe. For those of us who fail to grasp this, just divide our lifespan (even at a generous count unlikely to exceed 90 years) by the age of the universe (believed to be 13 billion years) and our true worth becomes apparent. Or consider our body mass, and the mass of all our possessions combined, as a fraction of the entire universe, and we quickly realize our feebleness. We may create something in our lives and believe it to be significant, but on a universal scale we are too small even to be noticed.

Bearing all this in mind, the question arises; on what basis can we sensibly place our relationship with the entity that created this vast universe? Our real motivation for seeking spiritual equilibrium comes from the knowledge that we came from nothing and we are worth nothing, and without spiritual connection we are utterly worthless. With it, we at least have some merit to place in the scales in our favor.

B. Ignorance of the fact that life is a test

Placing our own lives into context within the vastness of the universe will prevent us from becoming too self-absorbed. Our struggles and our triumphs alike are part of a test in which we face two options; either to act in accordance with our faith, and ethical principles, or to allow ourselves to be tempted by illusory rewards that end up destroying us.

An example would be whether we should allow ourselves to be late for a business appointment, in order to spend time explaining something to our kids? Or should we delay the explanation, and risk sacrificing their upbringing to favor our business appointment? If we delay, we face another dilemma: should we make their education our priority when we get home? Or do we risk forgetting, because there are other, more pressing things?

C. Ignorance of Types of tests

The tests we face vary. Some are large, some are small. An example of a minor test is to speak the truth even in difficult circumstances. Whereas a major test might be facing a moral dilemma that challenges our faith, and that we can only overcome by choosing to sacrifice something of great importance to us.

In all cases, if we keep in mind the need to act in a way that pleases God, He will ensure that we pass the test, and that success follows us.

Do we rely too much on white lies?

When the choice we face is between lying to save our skin, or speaking the truth and being damned, lying is often the easier course. But it is easy to get into the habit of using lies as an airship; an airship takes us up easily, but lies do not supply enough fuel to carry us to safety. Therefore they frequently cause us to crash.

White lies are often the easy option to take, but they erode our respect for the truth. Avoiding them can be difficult. If we wake up late on the morning of an important meeting, and then further delay ourselves by taking a phone call we were reluctant to ignore, and then spend ten minutes searching for the car keys that have slipped down the back of the sofa, and we arrive at the meeting an hour late; what should we tell our board meeting? Do we explain all our morning's trials, and then endure the resentment and disbelief on their faces? Or do we soothe the situation with a calming white lie, apologizing for our lateness, which, we explain, was due to our shoe splitting on the way to the station parking lot, and our foot becoming soaked by the rain, giving us little choice but to return home to change? Apologizing profusely, we explain our reluctance to turn up with split shoes, and we are relieved at the laughter that absolves us.

Facing this scenario, how many of us would choose the truth and be damned option, rather than the simple white lie?

Test of our willingness to make sacrifices

If we are sincere in our commitment to reach spiritual equilibrium, we must be willing to make difficult sacrifices. Being reluctant to do so, or refusing outright, is a major obstacle to our progress.

We have to restrain ourselves from causing pain to others by careless speech in moments of anger. Such restraint is a test of our character, for it is easy and gratifying to hurt those near us by speaking harshly or out of vengeance. If we do not restrain ourselves we may later feel remorse, but it is far better to show restraint in the first place.

Donations to the poor are effectively sacrifices of money. But they need to be given with genuine goodwill if they are to count in our favor. Simply handing over money, on the assumption that God will see what we are doing and reward us, is not going to advance our spiritual equilibrium, because it is not sincere.

Practicing religion can be seen as a sacrifice of time and mental energy. Dressing decently, and acting modestly, are also sacrifices, showing our willingness to sacrifice present pleasure in order to secure a better status in the next life.

These are just some of the many sacrifices we need to make. But if we persevere with them they become habits that are easy to follow. They can even bring us satisfaction and a sense of tranquility, as we know that in due course God will reward us.

Being reluctant to donate money to charity is an obstacle to spiritual equilibrium, and is very damaging. Charity presents us with an opportunity to benefit and honor God's creations. God does not need or want our money for Himself – after all, our money comes from His gifts to us. But He does love to see us being generous to those who need it, and when we help our fellows it is an irreplaceable opportunity to honor God.

Anyone who claims to have faith in God must therefore demonstrate that faith by being generous. Since we reap what we sow, when we are in need ourselves we can then expect God to be generous to us.

The duty to make sacrifices tests us all, and no one is exempt. If anyone fails to see how they fit into this scheme they are simply not looking hard enough, and they need to make a greater effort to identify the tests – large and small – that are laid out in their lives.

Even the prophet Abraham was tested. In his old age, when he was ailing, yet had no children, he prayed to God and God blessed him with a son. When his son was a young man, God ordered Abraham to offer up his life. Abraham showed his willingness to comply, by preparing the son he loved as a sacrifice. But God intervened and ordered him to sacrifice a ram instead.

By his willingness to perform even the most onerous of tests, Abraham showed he had reached the highest degree of piety and devotion to God. We therefore find that Jews, Christians and Muslims alike all revere him. When we look for the secret behind his honor and glorification among all nations, we find a clear relationship between willingness to make sacrifices, and being held in high regard.

E. Ignorance about the messages of our Creator

The third type of ignorance that obstructs our path to equilibrium is ignorance of God's messages to us. The prophets who brought us God's messages are all now dead, but God is everlasting, and He continues to speak to us through His actions. When our lives are good He is blessing us, and when they are hard He is warning us to mend our ways. If we heed these warnings, we can avoid far greater calamities. But if we ignore them the calamities will tighten their grip.

By now we should have realized that such calamities are beyond our power to avert, except through paying attention to the messages they carry and improving accordingly. We cannot expect other people to interpret events for us; we must each look into our own hearts and see where we are going astray. We should read and re-read Gods words, and re-evaluate our approach to life. If religion was not our guiding light when taking decisions, we should adopt it, asking ourselves each time we act, "Is this in accordance with God's will?"

In the Qur'an, God says: "And We have broken them (i.e. the Jews) up into various separate groups on the earth, some of them are righteous and some are away from that. And We tried them with good (blessings) and evil (calamities) in order that they might turn (to God's Obedience)." Al A'araf 168.

If we believe that God exists, then we must also believe that He controls the universe, and the world we live in, and all that happens in them. Believing in God requires us to believe that nothing happens without his knowledge and his will; any evil we suffer is part of his bringing us back to the right path. Medicine is by its nature strong, and has the potential to harm those who swallow it.

Taking medicines from the pharmacy when you are healthy will harm you; likewise almighty God's actions. Though they are in themselves pure goodness, they can appear to bring us evil; but the evil is simply a bitter medicine intended to restore our health.

We should believe that everything we endure will lead to good, and we should learn to read the messages contained within God's actions, as ignoring them will obstruct our progress towards spiritual equilibrium.

F. Ignorance of the limits of our knowledge

It is natural at times to be hungry and require food; and it is equally natural at other times to be sated, and refuse food. We are not lying when we say we are hungry, and we are not lying when we say we are full. These apparently contradictory statements are informed by our circumstances, which is why they change.

Religion can be viewed in a similar light. To the non-specialist observer, religion contains contradictions. But to those who understand it well, religion's apparently contradictory texts are simply reflections of the different circumstances in which they were written.

Sometimes religious instructions seem ambivalent or obscure, as though God is being deliberately vague. Why this should happen is hard to understand, but since it happens in all religions it is probably accounted for by the special nature of religious writing. Ultimately, if the lord of the universe chooses to express Himself in ambiguous terms, there is little we can do but accept it. But we should bear in mind that not all God's messages are meant for us. He may be addressing future ages, of which He has knowledge but we do not. It may be that His words will be easily understood by the people living at that time, and will solve a conundrum they are facing, thereby strengthening their faith. Or it may be that we are being tested, to see whether the lack of clarity diverts us from our faith.

But the fact that we cannot understand some parts of the body of religious writing, does not mean we can logically reject the entire religion. We cannot understand much of the workings of our own bodies, and we cannot always understand why particular medicines work; but we do not reject our bodies, or abandon medicine, as a result.

Continuously pushing to understand details is a satanic plan to plant doubt in our minds. And the greater our doubts, the smaller our faith. Thus doubts are the opposite of faith; they are hurdles that prevent us reaching spiritual equilibrium. Repeating the earlier example of a lab rat, who are we to demand that we must be given all the details of God's great scheme? We are mere mortals, whose bodies live short lives before perishing, at which time our souls finally understand that God has blessed us beyond our worth. God has a universe full of angels to praise and sanctify Him, He does not need creatures of clay like us. Nevertheless, He has chosen to honor us with His attention, for which we should show due gratitude.

Signs We Are Reaching Spiritual Equilibrium

A. Accepting both good and evil

God determines the course of our lives; our wealth, our spouses, and our children. We should therefore be content with what He has given us. Being content when times are good is easy. But maintaining that contentment when things become difficult is more challenging. Few people manage to trust God when they are facing adversity, and even fewer actively welcome that adversity on the basis that they know God ordained it, and trust Him to see them through it.

Some people feel that they have a special relationship with God, and use that belief to sustain their faith during difficult times. They remain satisfied with God even in adversity, understanding and accepting that both good and evil are necessary parts of life. And that both happen for a reason.

An ability to approach both good and evil with equanimity is the jewel in the crown of spiritual equilibrium. It is the strongest possible evidence of having reached a spiritual balance, and it is the reward that spiritual equilibrium brings us. It shows an acceptance of the fact that God controls the universe, and that whatever happens, be it good or bad, it happens with His assent, and should therefore be accepted.

God only wants good things for us. When we suffer evil, it is an unavoidable and transitory consequence, like an athlete suffering fatigue after competing. All our suffering will be rectified in the end. Similarly, when someone harms us they are acting as God's servant, according to His plan. It is not their free will.

Although we do not like being harmed, it does give us an opportunity to improve morally. It also strengthens us, and prompts us to review our life and count our blessings. And it brings us closer to the day when we dedicate our lives to God, and trust Him, and come to reach the spiritual plane that allows us to treat both good and evil with equal composure. When we reach that stage, we shall have been blessed with an ability to see things from a wider perspective, that makes us more content, and replaces our fears for the future with a sense of tranquility.

B.Carrying out hidden acts of righteousness

Spending time and money to help another person without expecting a reward in this life is a clear act of faith, and a sign that you are getting closer to spiritual equilibrium. Whereas the person who makes an ostentatious display of giving to charity in public, but hesitates to do so in private, should ask himself whether he is giving from the heart or simply for the public recognition.

C. Enjoying everlasting success and achieving dreams

Attaining spiritual equilibrium brings with it the reward of being blessed. Having faith in God, and acting consistently in ways that please Him also results in being blessed. For these reasons, angels are blessed, because they worship God consistently, and God is pleased with them.

Failing at times is natural. There is no shame even in failing repeatedly. Nevertheless, when God loves someone and approves of them, He guides that person, and makes others love him too. When someone fails repeatedly - fails to make friends or to find love, fails to make sufficient money to live on, despite their best efforts; whose family falls apart and who is left bereft – it is hard to see God's approval in such a person, for it is plain they have not been blessed.

Yet there are many people who do live blessed lives. Some are rich, others are poor, but what they all have in common is that in time their hopes are realized, and their lives are fulfilled. They bring to mind God's words "And verily, your Lord will give you all (i.e. good) so that you shall be well-satisfied."

D. Communicating with God by heart

Some people think of God only in a crisis, while others never stop thinking of Him, constantly asking themselves "Will this action please God?" or "How can I get closer to God?" When misfortune strikes them they ask "Why does God want me to endure this? What lessons does He want me to learn?"

The more we think of God and speak to Him in our hearts, the closer we get to Him. After many years of conversations with God, and of slowly climbing the stairway toward spiritual equilibrium, we come to understand just how much He has favored us, and the blessings He has bestowed on us. We recognize that it is God who sends us our wealth, and hears our prayers, and answers them. Only with this understanding will we stand before Him as followers, and read His words as admirers. At that time, the act of worshiping God will change. Rather than being driven by an anxious determination to get close to Him, our worshiping will be suffused with feelings of relief and tranquility. And for a lucky few, it will become a source of genuine delight.

E. Receiving people's love

Being loved by the people around us is a sign of having reached spiritual equilibrium, because when God loves someone, His creatures will also love that person.

This love stems from the positive attitude that a believer displays towards strangers, which itself stems from the influence of God's love. God's loves brings refinement and fairness, and a positive internal equilibrium that shows itself in the purity of that person's feelings. When someone's feelings towards other people are pure, and touched with humanity, those others cannot help reciprocating. This is the essence of spiritual equilibrium.

Chapter 3: The Equilibrium Machine – our brains

If the mechanism that controls our mental processes is disordered, what chance do we have of achieving equilibrium? Just as a shortsighted person cannot hope to see distant objects without their glasses on, we cannot hope to achieve equilibrium if our brain is not functioning properly, as it is our brain that guides us towards equilibrium. It achieves this by recognizing errors and leading us to solutions, detecting imbalances and steering our mental processes back to equilibrium.

The basic function of our brains, and those of other creatures, is therefore to maintain stability and order, and to avoid errors. When our brain detects an error or an imbalance, it searches for a way to correct it and restore order to our processes. We can picture the brain as an infant beneath the dome of our skull, that only thrives when we nourish it with knowledge and quench its thirst with experience.

Getting to know our brains

Structure of our brains

The human brain contains billions of neurons, whose job is to act as the electrical connections that form the basis of our memory, thought, empathy, voluntary and involuntary movements, and many other functions. These cells are connected to one another by links that we create as we experience events. When we walk past an alley or a neighborhood that we passed when we were young, it will remind us of events or experiences that are connected to that time and place. These memories are brought back to us because of the links our brain has formed.

Recalling one or two such places or events can lead us to recall associated experiences. For example, if we happened to be listening to a particular song at a certain place during our journey, and we now listen to that song again, hearing it may trigger memories of the place where we heard it previously.

This phenomenon arises because of the rule that our brain cells follow - "cells that worked together link together".

How our brains work

Our brains have stopped growing by the time we reach adulthood, but they never stop forming associations between neurons (our brain cells). These links continue forming into old age – as they are the way we create memories, and just as importantly, the way we form other types of associations. For example, we may become accustomed to drinking coffee in the morning, and feeling lifted by it mentally. This causes a link to be formed in our brain that associates coffee in the morning with a mental lift, and we look forward to the experience as a positive one. Whereas other people who have not formed that same association do not experience the same anticipation.

Because of the power of this linking process, we need to ensure that the associations we create are healthy ones. Forming associations that are based on misconceptions, or on wrong assumptions, can be harmful to our interests. For example, convincing ourselves that the grocer near to our house is expensive may compel us to travel a long distance to buy groceries, and end up spending more time and travel cost than we need to. Or, we may convince ourselves that the color blue does not suit our skin tone, and therefore automatically avoid buying all blue clothes; even though some shades of blue might suit our skin if we looked into the matter more deeply.

These are whimsical examples, but such associations can cause significant harm. For example, if we decide that our boss is hostile to us because his manner is always gruff when we greet him, we may become hostile in return and end up losing our job, or stressing ourselves unnecessarily with worry. In fact, looking deeper into the problem might tell us that our assumption is wrong, and that if we approach him in the right way he ceases to be gruff. All we need to do is improve our social skills to prove the association wrong and restore our equilibrium, rather than fleeing from the situation.

The importance of the associations within our brains

When we are born we are gifted the ability to create associations within our brains. Based on the associations that we form, we each create our own scale by which to judge issues. Some people stick rigidly to that scale, never deviating from their own opinions and never admitting that they are wrong, or that someone else may be right. This monopoly on the truth ensures that if anyone has a difference of opinion with such a person, they remain firm in their belief regardless of the evidence. Even if they are brought to court, they will insist that the truth is as clear as a sunny day.

This is why courts have existed since the dawn of civilization; because such people do not allow their beliefs to be inhibited by anything as inconvenient as the truth, or reality, and will stick stubbornly to falsehoods. Their inability to admit the truth allows them to fight to obtain property that does not belong to them, and I've noticed that they manage to adjust their morals to suit their own interests. When their lives fall apart no amount of advice can help repair them.

How do our brains operate?

Asking the right question

The key to understanding our brains is asking the right question. When we were young we didn't appreciate the immense power of the brain machine we carry around in our heads, and we didn't understand its outstanding abilities. We used to play with the machine like a child sitting in the cockpit of a aircraft, pressing buttons at random and asking Why? How? When? We heard the rumble of the engine, but we lacked the understanding to construct a proper sequence of questions that would make our brains fly.

Sequence of questions

A proper sequence of questions is one that elicits answers that expand our knowledge and open our minds. Each question should lead logically to another. We cease being fed answers at nursery school age, because the only way to learn about life is to grapple with issues and cope with hardship. Rarely in life are the issues confronting us simple.

Many of us love our morning cup of coffee or tea. We drink it habitually, without asking whether it is good for us or not, because such questions are not straightforward to answer, and require complex analysis. "Good" or "bad" for us are not simple concepts either, because a certain amount of the drink may be good and a larger amount bad. Or it may be good for some organs and bad for others, or good if drunk short term but bad if drunk long term. The complexities are endless.

To assess the health effects of actions such as repeatedly drinking tea or coffee requires us to apply our great brains to a detailed analysis of the relatively few facts available. Making us alert in the short term is just one effect of tea and coffee; the drinks also have other impacts. To understand the whole picture requires further and deeper research. If this research concludes that coffee or tea are harmless as long as we don't drink too much, we can then move on to the second question "How many cups of coffee or tea is too much?"

The question must fit the research. Some people might mistakenly ask "How many cups of coffee do I need to stay awake and avoid yawning?" but this is a different issue. Our research is looking into the health benefits of the drink, whereas the second question is looking into how effective it is at keeping us awake.

Differentiating between the two questions is the difference between a creative person and a loser. A creative person makes their brain revolve along the axis of their long term and short term benefit, until it achieves take-off and soars into the sky of their creativity; whereas the loser applies the vast power of their brain to short term benefits and hedonistic pleasure.

Simple questions added together produce substantial answers. The difference between aiming a rocket at the moon and hitting, and aiming a rocket at the moon and missing, can stem from just a minor deviation in angle, a slight mistake in the early planning stage, that becomes magnified each time a new calculation is based on its insecure foundations. Just one wrong assumption or missed question can see our rocket hurtling past the moon into darkest space.

Benefiting our long term health without sacrificing our short term interests is our ultimate goal. If coffee benefits us long term, while also stopping us from yawning and keeping us active in the short term, then all the better. But the question we should be asking is "How can we stop yawning without doing any long term harm?" In addressing it, we should construct a sequence of questions that examines the impact of coffee on our lives.

Understanding ourselves is crucial if we are to make accurate decisions. We need to be aware of our desires and our emotions, and recognize that they affect our decisions by pulling us towards short term comforts. Given that the future will one day be the present, and we will live then in a world as real as ours today, why not invest in it?

Some people take decisions that serve only their short term interests, and when the future arrives they try to find quick fixes without worrying about whether they are long term solutions. A sensible person is one who learns from others, while a wretched person is one who doesn't learn even from himself.

The design of our brains

Our brains are designed to learn, which means to acquire knowledge. The course of our lives and the things we seek both affect how our ability to learn develops. Some people focus their energy on bodily pursuits, and on satisfying their physical desires. These people apply their learning abilities to finding ways to relax and entertain their body. Other people focus their lives on the pursuit of money, and these people use their learning ability to find ways of maximizing their assets. While others make the soul their first concern.

We should carefully consider what we are focusing our attention on. By focusing on one aspect of our lives, we are forced to ignore another. So we should ensure that the things we focus on are those that are truly important, and the things we ignore are less important.

If someone helps his neighbor, but the neighbor responds with bad feeling, claiming that the good deed was done from an ulterior motive and refusing to offer thanks, the benefactor will feel hurt and slighted. But the person who devotes his life to improving his brain, and who loves learning for the sake of it, will gain something even from such an experience. He will look at the neighbor's bad conduct from an angle that other people would not think of, and he would recognize that he has increased his knowledge about his neighbor and learnt an important lesson about people. This would please him, and mitigate the hurt and frustration that the neighbor's behavior would otherwise have caused.

Such lessons are to be found in all bad experiences; it is just down to us to spot them.

The key functions of our brain

Decision making

A decision is the product of choosing, and an ability to choose is what makes us human. The choices we have made as a species have resulted in the prosperity and advancement that we enjoy today. While on a personal level, our lives are filled with choices, each of which is an opportunity to learn. Taking this opportunity and learning to make wise choices can affect our lives profoundly. Therefore it is important that we recognize the ability that our choices have to impact our lives, and the lives of the people around us, in the long term.

Whether taking major decisions at the top of the ladder, or minor ones down on the lowest rung, everyone makes choices. Whether business decisions or personal ones, we each make countless decisions every day. We may not realize the weight and long term effect of these decisions because we do not have time to place most of them under a microscope.

Nevertheless, it has been shown that small choices, often made subconsciously, can have significant effects. Researchers[7] have discovered that the causes underlying obesity include two hundred separate decisions about the type of food to eat at a given meal, its quantity, its preparation, how long it is chewed, and many other matters. If all these decisions arise from the simple act of the eater sitting down to dinner with his or her family, how many other important decisions affect our lives each day? And how many of them are made wisely?

Our decisions – large and small

Our large decisions are the major choices we make that have long term implications for ourselves and our families. If we decide to educate our children privately, it may consume perhaps half our annual income;

---

[7] Brian Wansink, Jeffery Sobal, Cornell University, 2007. Environment and Behavior. Mindless Eating:The 200 Daily Food Decisions We Overlook, 39, 106-123.

enough to make us consider the investment carefully, and to consider other options. We might also hesitate to take out a mortgage to buy our dream house, because such a long term commitment scares us. Can we really afford it? Would we be overextended? What if an emergency arose – would we have the resources to deal with it? The long term is always uncertain, and we are afraid about what would happen if our income should fall. On the other hand, with house prices rising, the longer we wait to take the plunge the more difficult the decision will be, with our dream house becoming less and less attainable.

Even an average, single person's daily life is filled with decisions. When we become responsible for the welfare of others, whether through starting a family or running a business with employees, or holding office in a community, life becomes one endless chain of decisions weighing down our necks. We also have to factor in decisions about our health, investing our assets, and nurturing our relationships.

Nor can we afford to ignore the small decisions, as they are often repetitive and have a cumulative effect that also impacts our life. Thus monitoring the decisions we take, understanding their importance and considering their implications, are at the heart of good decision taking.

Indecision is in itself a decision

A decision is not just when we take a positive action. It can also include an omission, because failing to take an action can have just as much impact as taking one. If we fail to ensure that we sleep sufficient hours, we are affecting our health. If we fail to moderate our responses to work colleagues or family, we affect our relationships. If we fail to count the number of soft drinks we have consumed that day, or to check the ingredients of a tempting new sweet we ate, we affect our weight, and our blood sugar.

Our time is limited, which means that we have to prioritize between competing claims, deciding which are the most important for us to focus on and leaving the others to take care of themselves. This requires us to prioritize well or risk overlooking an important issue. For example, if we fail to monitor our sleep, but our sleep turns out to be an important factor determining our weight and the strength of our immune system, and we then become ill as a result, would we not regret failing to monitor our sleep?

The coffin of our decisions

As youths we had many choices, but because we lacked experience we made few real decisions. Growing older we began aspiring to achieve something with our lives, and therefore investing time and mental energy in our financial goals, social standing, and personal relationships that would enhance our opportunities. As we travel the road towards fulfilling our goals the years pass, our choices reduce, and we rule out those that do not advance our ambitions. At the end of the road lies our coffin, when all our decision making ends. When that happens, all that will be left to show for our time on earth will be the decisions we took while alive. The number of our children, the type of company we kept, our relationship with our Creator.

Realizing that one day we will reach the end of the road is important, as it puts our decisions into context and helps us choose wisely. Money brings a good life, but at the end of the day we leave it behind in the bank and it passes to our heirs. Bearing this in mind helps us focus on the things that truly matter, and apply the money to useful goals.

The decision to pray is also important, for on the day we die we will break open the moneybox of our accumulated prayers and carry them with us to our next life, where they will stand to our credit. Knowing this will encourage us to invest our time in prayer.

Being aware that the road comes to an end is therefore essential to making wise choices. If we are driving, and narrowly avoid a crash, the realization that we have come within seconds of our death is the sort of shock that often brings home to us how fragile is our existence. This focuses our minds on the need to choose wisely while we still can.

When we are young we have the privilege of choosing the subject we want to study, and the college to study at. Each time in life we make a decision, the options open to us are narrowed. For example, when we choose to eat a certain food, we determine which illnesses we will suffer. And when we set the criteria by which we will choose friends, we limit the company that we will keep. Ultimately, the decisions we take during our life unconsciously determine the place and circumstances of our death, and where we are laid to rest.

Reassessing the familiar

The cost of running a car is high, thanks to the cost of hire purchase or credit, buying fuel, and servicing. We therefore spend considerable time calculating the best option to suit our income, best fuel economy, and looking for gas stations that are cheap. But thinking about the issues facing us from different angles can result in better choices. For example, careful analysis might show that we would do better to buy a larger car, with higher monthly installments, and consuming more fuel, but enabling us to drop four people off on our way to work. This would save transport costs for the family, or allow us to get contributions from friends to whom we give a ride. Before taking a decision, therefore, we should ask ourselves, is there a better way?

It may be challenging to force ourselves to reassess familiar situations from a novel angle, but it can benefit us greatly. And in time it becomes easier, until it is almost second nature. When an overweight person takes up swimming and pursues it diligently every day, he soon becomes slimmer and fitter, and is surprised by the transformation of his body to a more muscular and attractive form. Likewise with our brains. Our brains contain over a hundred billion cells, and by exercising the brain we learn to use these cells more effectively, to learn faster, and tackle issues more efficiently; until eventually we are surprised by the genius that we find living under our skull. Using the capacity of our brain to the full will benefit us greatly, improving our decision making and our thinking skills, and helping us make better choices.

Testing the limits of our knowledge

A man boarding a ship carries enough food in his bag to last himself and his family for six days. Each day he pulls food from the bag, and he and his children eat, and thank God for the food.

He tells his children that buying food on the boat is very expensive, and he could barely afford the fare, let alone restaurant bills; but promises that on the seventh day of the voyage, before they disembark, he will let them eat in the best restaurant on the boat.

Six days pass, and on the seventh day the children wear their best clothes and head to the restaurant for their special meal. The father lives up to his promise, and lets them eat to their hearts' content. After desert, he asks the waiter for the check. The waiter tells him that meals in the restaurant are free!

Many people do not even attempt that last dinner, preferring to live sealed within walls of ignorance of their own creation. They believe they are happy in the place where they live, but they miss far greater opportunities out in the wider world that they could easily benefit from, if only their curiosity was greater.

We should test the limits of our knowledge. Once we have mapped out the high walls that hem us in, we should consider our lives, and our actions, and our friends, and all of their actions, and local events, and politics, and we should strive to increase our knowledge day by day. Because the fog of ignorance can be cleared away by asking the right questions, and by sharing problems with friends. Where necessary we should seek expert advice, even if we have to pay for it, so that can discover the extent of our ignorance. Then, having delineated the boundaries of our knowledge, we should picture the green shoots of discovery that lie beyond those boundaries, waiting to bloom into greater wisdom. We all fear the unknown and settle for the familiar. But we should not see our known boundaries as fending off monsters that lie beyond; we should see them instead as gateways to greater knowledge that can be ours if we find the courage to explore. The more willing we are to take risks, the better equipped we will be to face the unknown.

We should constantly battle against the urge to laziness and indifference, because these are the greatest causes of our remaining ignorant. By taking leaps in the dark we push back the borders of our knowledge. We should make the effort to complement our friend's clothing, even if we dislike giving complements. We should make the effort to talk to a stranger, even if we are shy. We should try walking alone, and sitting in a library for hours with no company beyond our chosen books. We should experiment with any experiences that are not beyond the law, because the only thing holding us back from learning is the red card we show ourselves when we feel out of our depth.

Focusing on our ignorance helps us improve

Though we must leap beyond the barriers of our ignorance, that leap should not land us in a pit; we should find out where we will land before we leap. For example – two people are walking at night along a road dotted with deep holes. Which will arrive at their destination first – the one who walks quickly, or the one who walks carefully? If we examine their methods, we find that the careful person recognizes the danger of falling in and strives to avoid it, while the fast walker believes he would survive a fall and takes less care. The difference between them lies in their beliefs; the careful person sees the risk of falling into the hole as the greatest danger, and is willing to sacrifice the speed needed to reach his destination quickly. While the fast walker minimizes the risk that falling in represents. These convictions color their attitudes to speed, and to the danger of the road. The fast walker will not succeed in reaching his destination if he breaks his legs.

Life presents similar challenges. It too has long dark roads dotted with holes, and it has added dangers in the form of ignorance about events that touch us. We understand so little about our health, and our mental processes, yet we rush towards our goals. If our aim is to achieve more than those around us, we should review our approach. Are we avoiding the pit of our ignorance, or rushing towards it? And will we ever know, before it is too late and we find ourselves hurtling into the depths of a chasm?

Success consists of excelling against our peers, and climbing to the top of the pile. But before rising too high, we should learn to balance ourselves with care, lest we trip and tumble down. We must locate our own holes in the road, as represented by our ignorance, and fill them in if they are many, or avoid them if they are few. Because our lives are like roads that we walk daily, and knowing the pitfalls along the way is the best guarantee of safety.

Where the pit is ignorance, knowledge is the bridge.

Applying what we learn

Once we have gained familiarity with our brain, and discovered how to learn, the time has arrived to apply the knowledge that we acquire.

Understanding our characteristics

Each of us has individual characteristics. These have the potential to make our health, psychological and social problems unique, in the sense that scientific theories may not apply to us without modification. If we are struck by a fever and find that the standard cure causes constipation, when we already suffer from severe constipation, should we take the cure?

This principle can be relevant to all our problems. There are people we dislike dealing with, even though we have acquired social skills; and there are things that benefit us, but disturb us internally. It is wise to understand the characteristics, overcome our worries, and leave the benefits to when we understand them.

I admired a story that came to me through social media, of how a monkey and an elephant were close friends. During a stroll together they came across a river they didn't know. The elephant said to his friend the monkey, "Do not enter the water until I discover how deep it is." Once the elephant had crossed the river, the monkey asked him how deep it was. "Only knee deep…" was the elephant's reply. Without hesitating, the monkey entered the river and almost drowned. When he climbed out he shouted at the elephant, "How could you say it was only knee deep?" "It only reached my knee," the elephant answered, "And you didn't let me finish…"

It demonstrates that everyone gives advice according to their own characteristics. Thus we should be aware of ours.

Respecting specialization

If you are not a carpenter then you should try watching a carpenter open the lock on a door and then install a new lock in less than ten minutes. Visit a tool shop and buy the same tools he used, and try installing the lock yourself. You will be surprised at how difficult it is. If you are tenacious and keep trying, you will probably end up spoiling the first door you try it on, and maybe the second, even if you are a quick learner. Eventually, maybe on the third door, you might succeed.

Despite this book being a call to learning, there are times when I suggest that you respect specialization and forget learning, because one lifetime is not enough to learn all the trades and professions you would need to master. Carpenters, blacksmiths, doctors and others are all essential to our existence, and time is too precious for us to waste it attempting so many roles. We each have our own field, and should stick to it if we want to excel.

What we buy from specialists is time

Consulting with a specialist is to gain the distilled wisdom of thousands of books, and hundreds of years of human experience. We may have financial capital, but that alone is not enough to guarantee a new commercial venture's success. First we need an experienced business partner, who has specialist knowledge in our chosen field. Most ventures end in failure, but a suitable partner can reduce the probability of failure from[8]. Only masters of the craft survive in the marketplace, because they have the knowledge that enables them to step carefully between the holes in the road that others fall into.

The same applies across our lives. Specialists exist in all fields, and by making use of their skills and knowledge we effectively increase our own achievements, by saving the time we would have to spend if we tried to manage alone. Paying the fees to consult them is therefore a wise investment. If consulting one specialist does not achieve our goal, we need to consult another. Short of spending years learning their craft or profession, there is no other way to obtain the expertise we need.

Balance between skepticism and trust

Questioning wrong assumptions

Have you ever tried navigating a car using GPS? It might tell you to take a road that has been closed, because its information is out of date. If so, would you take the road blindly, and crash? We must allow ourselves to be guided by knowledge, but we must also question that knowledge, rather than following it blindly.

Humanity today is floating on an ocean of scientific theory. But are all these theories necessarily good for us? We must doubt theories before applying them, and doubt them again after applying them, and always

[8] Forbes Entrepreneurs. 90% Of Startups Fail. https://forbes.com

remain open to the possibility that they are wrong. Sometimes we need to look for new theories, or just apply old ones in a new way.

Trusting our proven facts

After my masters studies I had a slipped disc in my neck. I knocked on every door to get a better understanding of my illness; I read many books and articles, met with many doctors and clinics, and travelled far and wide in search of an explanation for the severe pain. Because I refused to stay on pills, the road to learning was long and uncomfortable. During the course of it, I bought many devices to reduce my pain, but on bad days it was still too much.

Having consulted local doctors, I looked online to find specialists in my country. The website showed pictures of the doctors, and gave details of their specializations. I immediately arranged an appointment with one of the most experienced specialists, and was relieved when he told me that the problem could be alleviated by placing a special neck traction pillow between my neck and shoulder, and inflating it for ten minutes daily. After a while, he said, I would be able to reduce the treatment to once a week. He told me that I would have to buy the pillow from abroad. I bought three of these pillows, but at first I doubted their effectiveness, and stopped using them. But once I placed my trust in them again, the pain went away.

I have had similar experiences many times during my life, relating to many issues. My natural inclination is too skeptical, but cures are

161

ineffective if you do not place your trust in them. Placing trust in proven facts is the way to achieve good results; if we distrust the road we are taking, and it is the right road to take us where we want to go, we will simply turn away from our destination. Therefore, anyone whose nature is doubting – like me – needs to learn to trust the facts he has learned, and give them time to demonstrate their accuracy.

Increasing our efforts when we are sure

I was once told of a young man who was learning Karate, but after years of training he was still unable to defeat the old man who taught him. He complained to his teacher that there must be some technique that he was holding back. The teacher denied this, saying that the reason the young man lost was simply that he didn't try hard enough to win. The young man insulted his teacher, and called him selfish for not teaching all he knew. In reply, the old man told the student "Follow me now, and I will show you the secret that gives me the upper hand." He led the student to a bathtub filled with water, and told him to place his head beneath the surface. There, beneath the water, he would find the secret he was searching for.

The student placed his head under the water, expecting to see some secret revealed to him. When he realized there was nothing but water he tried to raise his head, but the teacher placed his hand on the young man's head and held him down. Twice the young man tried to raise his head to breathe, and twice the teacher held him under with a powerful grip. The young man realized he was going to drown, and gathering all his strength he forced his head out of the water. Furious with his teacher, he left, and did not return to training.

Two months later, the teacher came to his house carrying a gift to mollify him. The young man asked why the teacher had held him under, when he could have drowned. The teacher replied "You tell me how you managed to raise your head when I was holding you down?"

The student replied, "I knew I was drowning, so I gathered all my strength and forced my head up."

The teacher told him "That is the answer to your question. You will beat me when you try hard enough. If you fail to make the effort, you will not succeed."

Likewise in life. We face many obstacles that are severe tests of our resolve. Unless we gather our strength to the utmost, we will fail to overcome them. A half-hearted effort will not be enough. We should bear in mind that too much skepticism can undermine our resolve too, for we will not try at our maximum effort unless we are convinced that the effort is worthwhile. The more we believe in the theory underlying our purpose, the harder we will try.

Experimenting out of our comfort zone

Imagine that you have spent seven days climbing a world class mountain, and there are only three hours of climbing time left to reach the top. Just imagine how intensely you would feel about reaching the summit. Is it likely that you would dawdle when you are standing just below the peak?

Whatever our goal may be, our determination to achieve it should match that of the mountaineer three hours from the peak. To keep our goals in perspective, we should distance ourselves from our normal viewpoint, and view our life from a new angle. This is difficult, and requires an effort, but is worthwhile because it will help us understand where we stand and where we are heading.

If we watch people, we will see how they run their lives differently from us. If a man is conspicuously kind to his son (whereas we are strict with ours), but his son is unresponsive to the kindness, we should ask the father what viewpoint drives him to continue showing such kindness. He might tell us that his son has special needs for some reason, in which case the example he is setting would not be relevant to our case. Or he might simply reply that he believes that harshness destroys children's creativity. This is a viewpoint we might adopt, and try ourselves.

If our neighbor drives a long way at the weekend to shop in a supermarket that sells at the same price as our local supermarket, we should try to find out why he does it, and then emulate his experience and see whether it brings us any benefit. We may discover that the goods are identical, but that the distant supermarket is a much nicer environment, and a more pleasant place to shop. And perhaps then we would find that our children want to come with us, to enjoy the attractions there, and we will get a chance to spend time talking to them during the journey. If we know someone who can spend hours reading a holy book, we should ask him what he gets out of it, and how its contents affect him. And if we have a friend who is kindhearted to the poor, and volunteers to help the homeless, we should try to understand his or her viewpoint too.

Sharing viewpoints and being open with one another makes life better and more beautiful. It also leads to us taking better, more productive decisions.

Our decisions

Setting our goals

Living life without clear goals is like walking in the unknown, or traveling in circles that simply lead us into confusion. Whereas living with moderate ambitions or short term goals may make our lives seem easy in the short run, because it leaves us unstretched and free to relax, where all those around us are hurrying. But in the longer term, when we see others exceeding our modest achievements, and realize that they were running in order to achieve something with their lives, the pleasure we take in relaxing will diminish. In its stead, we will feel that we have wasted our opportunities. Where others excel, we lag behind, and our discomfort is intensified by seeing those behind us overtake us as they rush to meet their goals.

People often set ambitious targets, aiming far into the future. Many of us do this to some degree, sometimes consciously, sometimes unconsciously. In itself this is not odd, but it does become odd when the goals people set are limited to financial goals. Money alone is not sufficient to bring tranquility. Setting goals for each of our five equilibriums is the real key to success as human beings. Being concerned with money alone is a superficial conceit, driven by our instinctive greed. Having more money than other people does not make us better than them. What makes us better is having a rounded personality with equilibrium in all five of the dimensions that are essential to our lives. We must understand these five needs and set targets that encompass them all.

Setting goals and following a path to reach them is an easy concept to understand. There is no shortage of advice on how to achieve it; the nearest library is bound to be filled with shelves full books on the topic. Therefore there is no point in dealing with it at length here. It is enough for me to point out that we need to direct our lives with precision. If you dislike reading, or listening to audio books, then overcome that dislike to learn more about how to set your goals. It is, after all, an essential part of succeeding. Reading up on management techniques is our best chance for keeping our lives moving forward in a straight line. And the person who walks in a straight line finishes first.

Mending our weaknesses

If we have a limp, it is an obstacle that prevents us running as fast as we can towards our goals. Setting unrealistic goals is equally an obstacle. It is one we create without realizing, and which sets us up for depression when we fail to achieve them. Have you ever seen a patient lying in hospital with broken legs? Can he run in a race? Not until his legs are mended. Similarly, we cannot compete in life until we set goals that are realistic.

Mending broken parts of our life before trying to progress is an important investment for the future, because we cannot hope to succeed until we have removed the broken elements that hold us back. Can you imagine flying in a plane that has damaged wings? Or riding your motorbike fast on the open road, despite knowing there is a mechanical fault? Or even driving in the rain when your windscreen wiper doesn't work, and you can't see through the windscreen? Isn't it obvious that in each case, we need to fix the damage before travelling?

The same applies to our life. Whatever is broken, should be fixed. Regardless of how much time, effort and trouble it takes. Aiming to meet our financial, social and spiritual goals starts by fixing our metaphorical limps. We can't be pure in God's eyes when we cheat on our wives; fixing the cheating is the first step, and only then can we begin climbing the stairs towards spiritual equilibrium. We can't have strong social relationships if we fly off the handle and say harsh words as soon as we become angry. We must fix our temper first, and only then can we hope to

167

build relationships with worthwhile people. Identifying our obstacles and working to overcome them lets us progress much faster towards our equilibriums, and makes the journey safer, surer, and more pleasant.

Many people review the decisions they have taken. But not everyone knows how to do so profitably, in the sense of spotting the errors they have made. Our brain takes the decisions, and to assess them we need to step out of our shoes and look at them critically, from the viewpoint of an impartial observer. We should also monitor how well our brain copes with the decision making process. It is after all the machine that guides us to our equilibriums, and if it is not functioning effectively, how can we be sure the information it has processed is accurate?

The delusion of standing above the center of facts

Our brains can be inflexible. When we examine our thoughts, our brain may refuse to cooperate with our search for flaws in our internal logic, because it instinctively works on the basis of assumptions. It does not want to countenance these assumptions being wrong, because to do so would require it to reassess all the basic ideas that allow us to function.

Imagine that we decide to buy a new house in a certain area, and then a friend informs us that it is impossible to live in that area because it is a very noisy neighborhood. Our brain will marginalize his words, and diminish them. Not because they are unimportant, but because to accept them would mean losing too much money, since we have already paid the deposit to the vendor. We might discuss the subject with him, but only on the basis of seeking to minimize his opinion, because we do not want to lose our deposit and we do not want to incur the trouble of searching for a new house. And perhaps we really like the house, and are pulled emotionally towards living there. With all these arguments running counter to his advice, will we listen to him, take a logical decision, and begin trying to recover our deposit? Or will we ignore the fact that there is a flaw in our plans, a metaphorical limp that needs to be fixed before we can run?

Our brain won't help us identify flaws in our thoughts. To the contrary, it will try to affirm our original decision, because although we want to get to the heart of the truth, we always seek comfort and ease over the stress that comes from searching for and finding mistakes.

But choosing comfort over the truth will send us down the wrong path in life. In the long run constructive doubting saves our time and benefits us. Whereas following our blind convictions gives only short term comfort, that rapidly changes to discomfort when we realize that we have been wasting our time and our peers have achieved more than us.

Excluding choices

When we limit our choices by determinedly excluding a particular path, are we doing the right thing?

Some people refuse on principle to discipline their children. But if the child does something wrong, and is not disciplined, how will they learn to follow rules? Or to behave in an orderly and socially acceptable way? Some people ask for their rights, but refuse to show anger. Instead, they present themselves as all soft and smiley. But part of demanding our rights is to show that we are uncomfortable without them, so that the person responsible for withholding them clearly understands that we are being oppressed. Some people do not want to deal with a particular person, or buy from a particular supermarket, or go to a particular hospital because of a previous bad experience. But is it truly in their interests to avoid that choice, or has their emotional center limited their options by showing an irrational red card?

We often reject particular choices because of an emotional objection, rather than a rational one. This simply demonstrates that our life is not balanced; but how often are we aware of the mistake we are making?

Analyzing our decisions

In the 1970's and 1980's, American management consultant Albert S. Humphrey applied and popularized SWOT analysis, a management tool for studying the four constituent elements of decision making. By studying these elements, a decision maker can tell where a decision will lead to in the future. The four elements of the decision making process Humphrey identified are: strong points, weak points, probable threats, possible opportunities to benefit.

For example, if we decide to change our job, we might consider the strong point of the new job is that it pays better; but the weak point is that the working day is thirty minutes longer. The danger associated with the new job is that the company is recently established, without the history and reputation of our old employer. It therefore has a higher risk of failure, as many new companies fail. It is also located far from where we live, and the road to commute along is heavily congested, which will further lengthen the day. The opportunities are that it will offer a greater chance of promotion, because the other employees are less experienced.

After setting these points out on a sheet of paper, we can repeat the exercise with the old job on another piece of paper, and compare the two to decide which is more attractive.

By adopting these four elements as an intrinsic part of our thought processes, we can better predict the outcome of our decisions, and make them more logical and less emotionally driven.

Obstacles in our minds

We all make mistakes, without exception. But whereas we try to correct the things that we do wrong, or say that are wrong, we do not spend time trying to correct mistakes in our thoughts. This is because it is easy to tell when we have said something wrong, just from the reaction we get from the people listening. And it is often easy to tell when we have done something wrong, because a friend will warn us that we are making a mistake. But it is much more difficult to spot when we are making a mistake in our thoughts. It is also difficult to correct such a mistake when we do spot it, because correcting our thoughts requires a high degree of self-awareness.

A popular Arabic saying holds that we are all fulfilled within our minds, but we never find fulfillment with our money. This is a good indication of the problem and its origins. It is our brains that control our actions, and are responsible for the things we do. Therefore fixing errors in our thoughts and in our beliefs will prevent us doing or saying things that are wrong, and will make us better people.

I was impressed by a saying I heard years ago that "All mistakes stem from our thoughts; so he who is mistaken in his actions does know not how to think." Many people fail to review their thoughts. This might either be because they believe that errors in thought indicate stupidity, and therefore refuse to countenance the idea; or because they just don't have the analytical ability. The belief that errors in thought indicate stupidity is patently untrue; the perfect human does not exist, and we all make errors in our thoughts. Hopefully, for anyone who thinks that way, this book can set them on the right path and encourage them to analyze their thoughts to identify the obstacles within their mind that prevent them achieving equilibrium.

Equilibrium is the brain's default position, in the same way that the universe has been constructed to achieve a state of balance. If we find that we are not thinking clearly, we must look for the obstacles within our mind that are preventing us achieving the equilibrium that should come naturally.

These obstacles may include:

1. Our emotions

Our emotions are the most important obstacles to equilibrium, because they interfere with rational thought. If, when raising our children, we only look at them with kindly eyes, we will fail to educate them in a balanced manner. Therefore, though our hearts may be overflowing with parental love, we override our emotions and take care to discipline them and instill proper values. Even though at times this requires us to be harsh, or to punish them.

The idea that punishing our children is wrong, regardless of what they do, is an obstacle in our mind that results from an excessive amount of emotion, not from any inherent correctness of the belief. Letting children grow up without discipline would make them wild and ill-behaved, and would cause us great pain when we see their misconduct. Even as we love and cherish them, we would know that they were bad. This would undermine our tranquility, and disturb our sense of inner equilibrium.

The way to avoid our mind leading us astray is to identify the centers within our brain that should be used to take decisions. As we have seen earlier, the emotional center is only one of the brain centers, being active when we experience moods such as happiness, fear, love and hate. The logical center is the part of our brain that calculates costs and benefits, carries out mathematical processes, and analyzes other logical processes.

Understanding the different functions of these centers and using them at appropriate times will help us differentiate between emotionally driven decisions that bring us short-term comfort, and logically driven ones that bring long-term benefits. If we find that we are too emotionally active to take an important decision on a logical basis, we should postpone taking it.

No one can completely exclude emotion from their decisions. But our logical center takes better decisions, and should be the focus of our decision making process.

If we think about taking a loan, it is impossible to avoid worrying about the repayments, and the lawsuits that could be filed against us, and the fate of the people who rely on us, as well as the people we would be spending the money on. All these are emotional issues. But there is a logical component to the decision too, and this should also be addressed. If we take some paper and write down all our emotional objections to the loan, the things that could happen to prevent us repaying it, and the consequences that could follow, we can then write next to each one the solution that can be devised to deal with it. For example, taking the loan from a different source with less strict penalties for non-repayment, or getting an extra job in the evenings to cover the repayments. These solutions are derived from the logical center of our brain.

Similarly, if an emotionally driven person is late repaying, and fears a lawsuit, he may become depressed. Whereas if a logically driven person is late repaying, he will be proactive in looking for ways to raise money, because he knows that whereas grief won't pay off his loan, action can.

The fuel of wrong assumptions

Returning to our earlier example, we might believe that raising our children without subjecting them to discipline is the right way to treat them. But we should realize that this is an emotional position, resulting from our parental love, not from any logical basis. In fact, it is completely wrong. If we raised our children without discipline they would be utterly unprepared for the outside world. Raising children without discipline would result in anarchy, both at home and, ultimately, for the nation. It would be like living in a country where prisoners are released onto the streets and lawlessness is rife. It would not benefit the children, who would grow up without learning the self-discipline necessary to get along with other people. And it would not benefit society.

There is a difference between a comfortable decision, and a good one. Emotionally driven people use their emotional center to take decisions that keep them within their comfort zone, but which may not be in their best interests. The 'comfort zone' being the feeling that arises from sticking with safe choices that we are used to, and therefore comfortable with, rather than experimenting or taking risks.

A preference for staying within our comfort zone governs many aspects of our lives. We stay in a unrewarding job, because we are comfortable with it, and afraid of risking leaving for a better one. But if our logical centre takes over we realize that we are wasting our time in a job that is unrewarding, and we will swap short term comfort for long term benefit and start looking for something better. All jobs have advantages and disadvantages; the logical solution is to assess the benefits of leaving our job against the benefits of staying. Or we could use some of our vacation time to try out the new job, and see if we like it.

Emotions affect our financial equilibrium through their impact on our work, and it is easy to see how emotions also affect our social equilibrium in many ways. When we become unforgiving of another person's mistakes, and remember their wrong every time we deal with them, it is emotion that is responsible for our intolerance. Logic would remind us that we all make mistakes, and that we would have better social relations with other people if we were forgiving rather than intolerant.

The effect of emotion on our health and internal equilibrium is also clear, as is its effect on our other equilibriums.

Emotions obstruct our productivity

Our emotions drive us to try to make decisions easier and less demanding to take. Because searching for the information needed for a good decision is time consuming, we often need to decide based on probabilities rather than thorough research. Since preparing for every eventuality is expensive, in both time and money, it is easy to see why people who allow their emotions to govern their decision take bad decisions and mismanage their lives. When emotion drives decisions it fails to differentiate between fact and assumption. It is emotion that makes people perpetual victims of circumstance, that tells them their mistakes are understandable and can be overlooked, and which clouds their understanding of reality. And when they turn away from everyone around them, complaining that 'no one understands their problems', it is emotion that is driving them.

Emotions obstruct change

Maintaining the five equilibriums requires that we adapt as circumstances change. But emotion can prevent us achieving this. To make friends we need to take the plunge and meet people, and then make the effort to get to know them. But this requires an investment in time and mental energy, and there is no guarantee that this investment will bring a return. We may be rejected when we attempt to develop the friendship further. Or we may find it difficult to get close to others, because we are impeded by our emotions, which find closeness threatening.

Our emotions stop us adapting by making us reluctant to step out of our comfort zone. This harms our future prospects, because change and progress in our lives are essential. We need to meet new people even if we find it threatening, and we need to try out business ideas even if many are doomed to fail. The short term discomfort that these actions bring is amply compensated for by the long term benefits; like a trip to the dentist that is painful at the time, but results in a cure for our troublesome teeth.

Yet we often avoid going to the dentist for fear of the pain. And likewise, we often avoid necessary changes for fear of the emotional strain they engender.

When someone criticizes a habit we can't get rid of, our emotions marginalize the criticism, telling us that it is wrong, even though logically we know it is right. They do this because the cost of addressing the bad habit is too daunting for us to face. But it is only our emotions that impose this cost on us, by weighting the equation against change. Our rational mind knows that change is needed. Too often it is the emotional center that wins, and the brain resists necessary changes. In the long run this harms us, because the higher cost comes from holding on to the past and not from changing.

How emotions work

Understanding the relationship between logic and emotion is very important. Emotion is the brain's fuel, because when we are uncomfortable we spend time thinking about why, and when we feel pity or some other emotion towards a person, we spend time thinking about them. To reach decisions that are properly judged, we must not let our brain be influenced too heavily by emotion, because emotion will drive us towards revenge when we feel angry. Then it will drive our brain to search for ways to implement this revenge. Instead we should ask ourselves rationally; what benefit will come from taking revenge?

Emotion makes us part ways with someone who appears to be bad or to lack loyalty. We find that we are averse to dealing with them, or having any contact with them, and we avoid them. Whereas logic tells us to bide our time, learn more about them, and acquire the skills and knowledge to deal with them. Eventually we may then discover that they have been bad to us, but very kind to other people, and that there is a reason for their behavior towards us.

There is a rich reward to be had from dealing with people that we would prefer to avoid, in that it teaches us valuable social skills. It is social skills that allow us to restrain others when they are threatening to encroach on our territory, without engaging in a fight, and without triggering negative emotions that will antagonize them and cause them to encroach even further. Social skills also help us understand that their encroachment comes from the fact that people rarely see other people's boundaries, because they are too busy concentrating on their own affairs.

Emotions pull us out of our roles

Emotion incites us to get involved in roles that are outside our competence and responsibility. Imagine that a beloved relative falls ill, and we assume responsibility for helping him. If the illness is a long one, we are at risk of confusing our responsibility for helping him, with responsibility for curing him, which is not within our competence. Because of our determination to see him recover, and because our brain's emotional centre has assumed responsibility for his welfare, we act emotionally rather than logically. Logic would tell us to do what we can to help him, but that we should leave the rest for the Lord of the Universe to determine. Because our brain's emotional center can't differentiate between our responsibility and our wish to see the person healthy, we wrongly assume responsibility for curing him. And if his health declines, we blame ourselves for failing to discharge an imaginary 'responsibility' that we did not have in the first place.

Emotion is both a power and an obstruction

Emotion is responsible for obstructing our path towards equilibrium in two ways. Firstly, it has the potential to prevent us taking a balanced approach to issues, as in the example of a belief that children can be raised without discipline. Secondly, it magnifies our fears and causes us to worry incessantly, thereby wrecking our internal equilibrium.

Emotion can also be beneficial, and serve to strengthen us. It drives us to work harder and motivates us to excel. And in the case of love, one of the strongest emotions, it motivates us to care for our families. We cannot erase our emotions, nor should we fight to suppress them. They are an essential part of us, and without them we would lose much of our vitality. But we must monitor them, be aware of their potential for harm, and ensure that they do not work against us by distorting our vision. Just as they can undermine our decision making, if our emotions run unchecked, they can also undermine the basis of our lives.

Avoiding inappropriate emotion

Avoiding being controlled by excessive and inappropriate emotion is the key to attaining equilibrium. When we are assessing an issue, before reaching a decision, we must rid ourselves of emotional influences that can distort our decision making process. Emotions try to bind us to decisions that satisfy our desires, rather than decisions that are in accordance with reality. To achieve this, we need to trust that our real benefit comes from taking rational decisions that are based on reality, not emotional ones that are inevitably clouded by short term considerations.

However, we cannot take decisions that avoid emotion completely. We need to distinguish between harmful emotions, and necessary, healthy ones. Imagine that our boss at work is malicious and nasty, but we refuse to accept this, because to accept it would mean that the only course open to us would be to find another job. So we ignore the clear facts and assign his hostility to anger and temperament, rather than malice. Yet there are genuinely malicious people in the world, and sometimes we are unfortunate enough to have as our boss someone who deliberately harms us. Perhaps because he wants to appoint one of his relatives in our place, or maybe we stand in the way of him receiving a substantial bribe. Therefore he decides to go to war with us.

A good natured person might take years to discover the truth about their boss, because their emotions prevent them from seeing clearly. A further reason might be down to their nature, which is too inflexible to alter their opinion in the light of facts. If this is the case they must challenge their nature, and overcome it, because it is not acting in their interests.

Think of emotions as ropes that impede our brain's freedom of judgment, thereby causing an imbalance. It is because emotions represent the distorting potential of our desires and feelings that judges do not rule in their own family's case. The closer we are to a decision, the harder it is to be impartial. But when it comes to issues within our own lives, we cannot stand aside, as judges do. We need to take decisions, but we need to do so with as much impartiality as we can.

2. False Assumptions - (i.e. imaginary truths)

Assumptions are the most damaging enemies of our mind's equilibrium. When we are convinced that we are too busy to exercise, and the doctor tries to convince us that exercise is essential, we may fail to realize that being "too busy to exercise" is simply an assumption not a fact. We imagine that we are too busy because of our failure to give a high enough priority to exercise. But when, in years to come, our organs fail because we have not looked after ourselves, and our arteries are clogged, and we are lying in a hospital bed, we will realize that we would have been far better off if we had given exercise a higher priority and found the time. If we then recover and leave hospital, we will miraculously discover that our assumption that we were too busy was wrong; as proven by the fact that we now manage to find all the time we need, in the hope that we can avoid another decline.

Similarly, although we now know that smoking is associated with lung or throat cancer, every smoker secretly assumes that they will be safe from the disease – although there is no logical basis for this assumption.

We make so many assumptions in life we cannot count them all. For example: "I'm educated so I don't need to read about this topic", or "I can trust this person, he is honest" (he may have been previously, but perhaps he has changed?) Or "A doctor is too knowledgeable ever to be wrong" (but what if he makes a mistake in prescribing our medicine?) Or, "I can't trust anything this person says, he is a liar," (he may have been previously, but perhaps he has changed?) "There is no point complaining, because no one will listen," or "He won't help me, even though I have often helped him", or "This person is shameless," (perhaps we just caught him at a bad time?) Or, "There are no jobs to be had," but perhaps we just haven't looked hard enough?

Assumptions are cheap and readily available building materials with which to construct a world of false certainty. Our brains rely on them because authentic materials are costly – if we made no assumptions, before we reached a conclusion about anything, we would need to research every issue in detail. Instead, we lay out guidelines in our mind, using assumptions as a scaffold on which to build complex theories. But the certainty of these assumptions is an illusion, which means that the theories we construct using them are unreliable.

In business, as in our personal lives, we seek to maximize our efficiency by making assumptions. But we simply undermine ourselves. The man who assumed he didn't have time to exercise built his life around that assumption, but had he been sensible he would have built his life around truths rather than assumptions. In this case, on the truthful advice of his doctors that he needed to exercise for at least two sessions a week. Rejecting truth for assumptions in the hope that it would help him earn more or build a bigger business proved to be a rash mistake, in which his priorities were shown to be misguided. The correct analysis for him to apply would have been that he didn't have time to be ill, and therefore he needed to take such measures as were necessary to safeguard his health.

An assumption is an imaginary truth. To avoid having to embark on a search for actual truths, we fall for these comforting illusions because our emotions convince us that they are genuine. Even though our logical center would recognize that they are not genuine if we only gave it a chance to speak. So, we choose comfort over truth, and end up being led astray.

If we assume that living our lives without lying is impossible, we will lie. Strangely, this is often welcomed and even encouraged. In the same way that we delude ourselves with false assumptions, people often prefer to deal with others who delude them by telling them what they want to hear, despite the fact that it is a lie. And since such lying is rewarded by popularity, it multiplies.

But the higher we build our edifice of falsehoods, the greater the risk that it will come crashing down. Which is why although most of us will lie in an emergency, a sensible person refuses to profit from deliberately sacrificing his or her principles. If we are forced to do so once, we will not repeat it; and if we are compelled to repeat it, we accept that we have transgressed out of compulsion and do not attempt to justify it.

Many people do justify their wrongs, and because they are in reality unjustifiable they cloak them behind false assumptions, such as "people want to be lied to, therefore it is acceptable" or "this is important, and it can't be done without a few lies." But a person who lives in a world of falsehood and deceit obscures rather than solves their problems. They confuse their lies with reality, and forget to search for real answers to the problems they are facing. Those who live by making assumptions will assume that lying is acceptable, and that people need to be lied to, and that there is no other way to achieve their goals. And their lives being built on false assumptions, they will end in ruin.

Differentiating between facts and assumptions

Life forces us to deal with people whose integrity is unknown to us, but in reality we have little choice but to assume that they will prove to be honest. Similarly, we have to assume that people whose truthfulness we have not tested will nevertheless prove to be truthful. Even the most skeptical and suspicious people have to make assumptions about these and other matters, even though there is a risk that these assumptions will prove to be wrong. The alternative would be to test every assumption before we act, and check that every fact is accurate, which is simply not feasible. Nevertheless, there are some pointers we can bear in mind, to make the process of differentiating between fact and assumption faster.

Paying attention to signals and ignoring warnings

Warnings are signals that tell us we are going wrong. If we pay attention to these warnings, we will then know to override our assumptions and check our facts.

Imagine that we are planning to drive a car in Europe. How different are the traffic laws? Every country in Europe has its own laws. The driver who goes there and habitually ignores blaring horns, and fails to ask himself why he is being beeped at, should therefore take great care. If he continues ignoring the horn beeps he will end up colliding head-on with the cars in Britain, as they drive on the other side of the road. The horn beeps may be annoying, but they are an early warning that foretells (and prevents) disaster.

Painful criticism is the same. Even if it comes from an enemy, it may still be sincere. But much better than waiting until we are openly criticized, we should be aware of the signals that precede it. Picking up on the subtle gestures and other behavioral signals from those around us will save us from the mounting pressure that leads to overt criticism.

We should in any case welcome criticism, as it alerts us to our flaws. If someone disrespects us, we should ask what we have done wrong? And we should return to that person later, to check whether they were simply speaking out of anger, or whether the criticism was meant fairly.

There are many warning signals in life. We need to build a repository of warning signals in our brain, to alert us to problems before they arise. A relative who changes their behavior towards us is sending signals that should not be ignored. If they decide to harm us, their daggers would be too close to avoid. The safest response is therefore to take a step back, and verify that the signals really do represent a behavioral change.

If a friend repeatedly jokes about the same topic, we need to analyze our repository of early warning signals to find the reason behind the jokes. If we can't find an explanation, we need to review the entire context when we have time for reflection. We may then find a nugget of helpful advice that has been cloaked in humor to avoid embarrassing or insulting us.

We may interpret the signals we see as confirming our incorrect assumptions. But we must remain open to the possibility that we are wrong, to avoid damaging our signal receiving mechanism. And be aware of the effect emotions have in distorting our ability to interpret signals correctly.

Setting priorities

We need to prioritize our efforts to examine facts according to their importance. We stand to lose relatively little by assuming that a grocer is honest, so testing the assumption is not a priority. But if we buy a house, and accept the assurance of the estate agent that the area is safe, we stand to lose twenty years' worth of income that will be needed to pay for the house, if it turns out to be untrue. Clearly therefore, we need to investigate the truth of the assurance as a priority.

Making sure of the standards at our children's local school is another example. If we uncritically accept an assurance as to the school's quality, our children may end up as drug pushing delinquents. Yet we may also assume that we lack the money to send them to a better school, and on this basis fail to properly investigate the local school.

We can't build a second floor without making sure of the stability and structural integrity of the first. Sending our children to a school is the first floor; the second floor is for them to complete their studies, leading to good job prospects.

Assessing the priority of an issue is the first step towards examining the facts. We need to bear in mind that hunting down information takes time and effort. And that time is money. If we want to know about a potential new school, we will have to research online, read blogs and articles, ask friends, ask neighbors…. All of which is time and effort that we could have devoted to other things. Ultimately, this could result in an even greater expense, if we find that the school is not good after all, and we have to enroll our children at a more distant school.

Being aware of the time, effort and cost that enquiries will require, increases the danger that we will try to save it all by making invalid assumptions. This would be the easier course for our brains, which love to cut costs and magnify results. But if we give in to the temptation to cut corners in this way, we will be building the second and third storeys of our lives on the shaky pillar of invalid assumptions.

Invalid assumptions create invalid links

People feel severe embarrassment at the thought of being shown up as wrong. Often they will avoid asking the person in front of them, to avoid being corrected, even though they are sure the person in front of them has the answer they need. They think that asking makes them students, and they want to be teachers.

There is a link between social status and learning; the more someone knows, the higher they are placed in society. For those who persist in the habit of not asking for information, to avoid staining their image, they are consigning themselves to languish on the bottom rung of humanity.

Because reaching the heights of social status is impossible without either knowledge, beauty, or guts.

Learning is hindered by many assumptions. We assume that a certain person is ignorant, therefore we ignore what they say. And we assume that reading before bedtime is impossible, because we are too tired; but have we actually tried? Likewise the assumption that the weekend is for resting, not learning; if we don't study at the weekend, when will we? And the assumption that learning ends once we have our university degree. We create these negative links in our brain, and they hold us back for years. Their effect becomes clear in time, when we compare ourselves to someone who is open to learning new things every day.

Wrong assumptions can be complex

Sitting at the dinner table with the family is not wise if we are trying to lose weight. We see our favorite dishes, but we are determined to make our diet succeed, and for a while we resist the temptation. This may last a few days, or a week, or even longer. But then the dam bursts and we gorge on everything we have been trying to avoid. We become annoyed with ourselves, and assume that our willpower is weak. But our assumption is wrong. The truth is that everyone is tempted by delicious food, and it was a mistake to sit at the table in the first place.

We make this invalid assumption about willpower because it is easier than looking deeply into the subject to find the truth. If we really want to understand willpower, and what factors determine its strength, we would need to read up on the subject and get specialist advice. Then we would understand why we really gave in to our hunger, rather than assume that it was a lack of willpower. But such in-depth investigation would be troublesome and inconvenient. So instead we just assume.

It is the need to save time and mental energy that drives us to make assumptions, and makes it difficult to wean ourselves off them. Breaking the habit requires an enlightened mind, and critical self-analysis of the way our brains determine the facts that underpin our life.

Facts change

Facts change over time, and vary from place to place. Determining them requires a lot of effort and energy. Re-examining them to stay up to date is even more expensive. Because our emotions are reluctant to expend the effort needed to keep up to date with changing information, we become frustrated and annoyed at the burden it imposes.

Cures are discovered for illnesses, but we remain unaware. Laws change, and our understanding of them becomes outdated. Prices fall, friends falter in their regard for us…Life is full of examples of evolving situations that require us to keep abreast. The worlds of business and finance are full of examples of major corporations which went under because they failed to keep up to date with changing circumstances.

To avoid following their example, we must constantly update ourselves, despite the exhausting effort this requires. What has been examined must be re-examined, what has been learned must be re-learned, what has been verified must be re-verified. The more we allow ourselves to become out of date, the more we distance ourselves from equilibrium.

The irritation that comes from having to spend time ascertaining facts such as the safety of our children's school, can be compensated for by the satisfaction of discovering that the school is good. This may be established by speaking to a recent graduate of the school, and verifying that their information is up to date.

Knowing when to delve deeper

We cannot examine every fact, therefore we need a way of judging which should be given priority for our limited resources. It is like when you buy an expensive device. You cannot buy every device on the market, so you decide carefully which device will bring you the most return for your money. But you need to have up to date information to make your choice. Choosing on information that was accurate six months ago does not guarantee that you will make the best choice today, because new models come out and the technology becomes cheaper. Buying an out of date, expensive model when there is a newer, cheaper version available is painful. Just as it hurts to spend money training for a qualification that no employer wants.

Replacing false pillars

As time passes, our beliefs evolve. We may discover that we disrespected someone undeservedly, because we were too intolerant. But in the fullness of time we mellow and become more forgiving.

This process of re-evaluating people can be costly. The mental effort required to reassess our beliefs can be intense, and it may be disturbing for us to have to approach them with assurances that we have recognized our earlier error and want to make amends. Because this is difficult we may resist, but this resistance must be overcome because it hinders us from making our peace with them. We need to muster the required patience and demonstrate that their skepticism is unfounded. When they see with their own eyes that we have genuinely changed, they will reciprocate.

In all things, we must dismantle our false pillars of belief, whether they be social, financial, internal or spiritual, and replace them with sound structures based on accurate information.

Assumptions destroy us

Many people surrender to cancer because they assume it has no cure. They start praying in preparation for meeting their Lord, or they devote themselves to pleasure to get the most out of what little time they have left, convinced that their life is over.

Others assume that psychological illnesses can't happen to them. When depression strikes it turns their lives upside down, and they decide to commit suicide. All because they wrongly assumed that psychological illness could never be their problem – but it is.

It is their false assumption that causes their suicide, not their depression. Depression can be cured, and sufferers can break free of it. But false assumptions have no cure, once we have adopted them and ingrained them into our psyche over a period of years.

3. Wrong goals

Allowing our emotions to determine our goals

When our emotions are allowed to determine our goals they set us objectives such as revenge, or domination of others, or a vain desire to achieve pre-eminence. These goals do not serve our interests, but the interests of our emotions. More useful would be to achieve control over ourselves, and to aim at constructive targets rather than at dominating our peers. Rivalry for its own sake does not bring us any benefit, but simply gratifies a desire buried deep in our brains.

If we obtain a high status in society by our academic achievements, will we then stop learning, because we have achieved our goal? It is not difficult to imagine a man who obtained a doctorate for the status it brings, rather than a love of learning, being publicly shamed; because after getting his doctorate he fails to stay current with fast moving developments in his field, and makes a public statement that is wrong. Having obtained the doctorate for a shallow purpose he has wasted his time, money and effort.

What leads us astray is that we set goals without analyzing our real needs. Once we delve deeply into our real needs, our true benefit over the coming years becomes clear, and so too do our true goals.

The trial of a person who murdered forty eight girls in the United States of America ended with a deal that required him to plead guilty and lead the way to the corpses of his victims, in exchange for life imprisonment. When he entered his plea, and came face to face with the relatives, insults were rained on him from fathers, mothers and brothers of the victims. The expression on his face was neutral, until an old man came to him and said that it was difficult to apply forgiveness as he learned from the Bible, "But today I forgive you." At this, the murderer broke down in tears.

The relatives had been driven to insult him out of a desire for revenge, and to shame him for what he did to their loved ones. All of which was understandable, and for which I cannot blame them. But I would question whether the goal of revenge actually benefitted them. More beneficial was the reaction of the old man in forgiving the killer of his daughter. This was an example of setting goals that serve us rather than our emotions, of applying the lessons we have learned in life, and breaking away from harmful emotions.

Beware of attaching emotions to goals

Chasing emotionally driven goals is a mistake no one is safe from. Our emotions are the motors that power our actions; but letting emotion determine our objectives will deprive us of the pleasure that comes from achieving them. The correct path is to determine our goals logically, and when we reach each goal, to simply set another one. If we make achieving our goal a pre-condition for attaining psychological peace, failing to achieve it will make us depressed.

We spend a large part of our lives chasing our goals, and when we reach them we experience just a fleeting moment of pleasure. I know people who become deeply emotionally involved in this chase, and endure years of sadness and pain in the hope of reaching them. By spending years of sadness to achieve brief moments of joy, we are just adding to the misery of our lives. We become no better than aquarium dolphins, entertaining thousands of spectators as they strive to earn the reward of a small fish that lasts just one bite.

As part of monitoring our emotions we need to consider the extent of the emotional commitment that our goals will demand. Is the brief reward that comes from achieving our goals really worth the effort required? Will the achievement satisfy us for long, or will we immediately launch into new objectives? Because our life is a journey, aiming at a target and focusing our energy on hitting it will not benefit us. We would do better to focus on the journey itself, and ensure that we derive pleasure from the ride by restoring our equilibrium and travelling in serene tranquility.

Searching for results

The road to results passes through failure and bitter experiences. Constantly working to identify our mistakes brings us closer to perfection, whereas constantly searching for perfection ends in failure. Therefore he who searches for a route to success is searching for a shortcut to failure; while he who searches for the reasons behind failure, is searching for the shortcut to success.

The following are the most important obstacles in our brains that come from searching for results:

Striving for labels

Dr. Carol Dweck in his book *Mindset: The New Psychology Of Success* identifies two types of minds. The first is interested in experiences and doesn't care about outcomes. It sees failure as a beneficial experience, and therefore it is interested in day-to-day events and achieves its goals by concentrating on experiences instead of outcomes. The second is interested in labels. It lives its life in pursuit of outcomes; it has no interest in day-to-day events and all that matters to it are outcomes. When it achieves one outcome, it moves on to the next. This mind is in pursuit of labels. It works with the aim of proving it is the best, and it learns with the aim of proving its excellence. It gathers certificates so that people will label it "educated", and it buys expensive things so that they will label it "rich". This way of thinking rules out outcomes that describe the person as ignorant or imperfect, because it is only interested in being perfect on the inside. It spends all its energy looking for ways to obtain labels that will appear to denote success. And if it should find that it is ignorant, rather than motivating it to learn, this de-motivates it.

Learning only happens when we admit we are ignorant. Therefore, a mind that is concerned only with labels obstructs the process of learning. Our goal should be to profit from every experience by gaining knowledge. By assuming that our mind is perfect we reduce our ability to learn, because a perfect mind does not need to acquire new knowledge. We therefore make ourselves unreceptive. If we view knowledge as a means to an end, we will learn less from each experience than if we view knowledge as an end in itself.

Searching for your comfort zone

I used to sit with my children discussing their problems. I would show them solutions to their existing problems, and try to teach them the way to find solutions to future ones. I would ask them, how does the brain work? And they would answer, as I had taught them, "With questions." Then I would set them a problem and ask "What questions should the brain be asking here?" They would try to think of the best questions to ask first, because asking the right question is the key to reaching the solution. The ability of twelve year old kids is no less than ours; we only exceed them in our experience of using our brain, while they are lost in the complexities of constructing the right chain of questions, which is 99 percent of finding the right answer.

The right question usually leads to another question, not an answer. Though we are searching ultimately for an answer, chasing answers directly leads to wrong answers rather than accurate ones. To find truthful answers we must replace the search for answers with the search for truth. To reach the solution to any problem we must ask the right question; overcoming multiple obstacles requires finding the right sequence of questions; and if we make a mistake in any part of that sequence, we will surely end up with a wrong answer.

Let's imagine that we are travelling to a two-day conference, and that our destination is hit by a snow storm. As a result the airport has closed. We land in a city 100 km away, and ask for directions and an idea of the time and cost of completing our journey. We then decide to continue towards our destination. But the one thing we forgot to ask, was whether the conference is still going ahead? Or has it been cancelled?

When we reach wrong answers, we must review our questions. Perhaps we failed to detach ourselves from our emotions when we asked them? For example, when a person we know changes, we can ask ourselves, "Why has this person become unpleasant?" We could also ask, "What pressures is he facing that have caused him to change?" Though the two questions are similar, the first one refers to our emotions. By framing the question in an emotional way, it risks reminding ourselves of past shared experiences when he was not unpleasant. In the process, it may distract us, and hinder us from reaching the right answer. The second question, however, is framed in terms of learning more about the person, and therefore understanding him better.

When we ask questions that do not lead to learning, we lead ourselves astray. We also fail to improve our brains and the mental processes we need to build our lives. Life becomes more complicated as we grow older, and those who refuse to build their mental capacities by educating and evolving their brains will shy away from its complexity, and therefore turn away from success.

When we ask the wrong questions, we are trying to influence our brains to reach outcomes that suit our desires. Such outcomes will not benefit us, because they are not rational goals but emotionally driven ones.

In Conclusion

Polish your jewel

We are so preoccupied with the detail of what is happening in our lives that we fail to learn from what we have experienced. Implacable problems grind us down and turn us into diggers tunneling blindly in the rocky terrain of unsolvable issues, while setbacks shrink our options and drive us along paths from which we can see no escape.

We should learn from experience to refashion ourselves to suit the terrain. Some of us have heads of steel, others of diamond, but whatever material we have at hand we should apply it to attack our problems in the best way we can. Sometimes we will succeed, other times we may fail. But in either case we will end up stronger for the experience, and better equipped to cope with future problems. So we should polish our digging head and prepare for the challenges ahead.

We discover our brain's buried abilities when we learn, and when we put our new knowledge into practice. Carefully analyzing the events in our lives can open our eyes to vast oceans of knowledge that we need to understand. When we see a needy person in the street we may push his plight from our mind, and assume he does not want to work. Or we may give him alms and engage him in conversation to understand how he views his life, and discover what he thinks of the city we all share. After learning what he has to say we may think about his life, and the challenges and setbacks that drove him to live as he does. Then we stand to profit from the encounter by comparing his life to ours, taking note of the dangers he suffered, and taking care that we avoid them.

We might also learn humility, compassion and kindness from talking to him. We might get into the habit of saying "Good morning" each day when we pass by. Or we might learn that he is a bad person, and avoid him.

Whatever we learn, the act of learning daily is important. It stems from the realization that learning in itself is a good thing, and necessary to our growth and development. The more we understand this, the more we will be committed to learning, and the more things we will find that are worth learning about.

Ride your horse

Even if you are lucky enough to have an easy life, one that is orderly, controlled, and apparently problem free, don't imagine that you are immune from the danger of finding yourself riding a bucking horse. When chaos strikes, just look down and you will see the horse rearing up beneath you, ready to plunge you headlong into danger. Because the life you are leading is just the calm before the storm. Or perhaps a hurricane has already hit you, but you are in the eye of the storm, skirting danger by the merest hairsbreadth, and haven't yet realized it.

Our lives are very complex. Misery preys on us night and day, and we must equip ourselves with deeper understanding and better skills to cope with the complexity and constant change that fate throws at us. Any time we are knocked down, we must quickly get back up, to find and deal with the mistake that undermined us. Then we can climb back on our horse, and take charge with a firmer grip and better character.

Reaching equilibrium in any issue simply requires stability in the face of change. Imagine you are back on that bucking horse, can you expect to stay on its back just by stabilizing your movements? Of course not. And in the same way, dealing with the instability life throws at us requires that we adapt ourselves to maintain stability and equilibrium.

If our salary happens to fall and we refuse to reduce our expenses, the outcome will be eroded savings, then debt. If we want to remain debt free we must change our lifestyle to suit our new circumstances. The faster we adapt, the closer we will draw to equilibrium.

It is true that cowboys can balance on bucking horses, and we can remain on top of life if we focus on maintaining our equilibriums. But life is more complex than riding a horse, because our needs evolve. What suits us today repels us tomorrow, the opportunities open to us change, our friends change, and some of them set traps for us. Therefore life is a constantly shifting arena that is filled with bucking horses and screaming, unpredictable spectators, and our objective is to maintain equilibrium so as not to fall. To keep a steady course towards our goals as life shifts the scenery around us, we have to adjust our compass and trim our sails.

Have you ever tried running while holding a cup of water? That is how life works; we carry our five cups in the tray of our days and nights - nestling within them our equilibriums for each of the five essential dimensions - and run with them towards our goals. We cannot stop, because we will miss our targets. Therefore we constantly try to fill them on the move. And if we do try to stop, life ushers us on, forcing us to jump through one hoop after another in search of food, and shelter, and wealth, while year by year we grow older and face decline.

We are all far from equilibrium

I don't know how old you are, dear reader, and I don't know your academic or professional background. I wish I could practice my hobby of deducing information about you, and your manners and successes – as I did with the long-haired man ordering coffee. What I do know is that no one gets full marks in all five equilibriums. Some exceed 80% in physical equilibrium, and 70% in spiritual equilibrium, but others fail to reach a good grade in any of their equilibriums. Our target should be to achieve exceptional grades in all our equilibriums. Therefore we must work on our ignorance; because the primary obstacle to achieving exceptional grades is ignorance.

Our innate tendency is to focus on what we know and understand, and ignore what we don't. But in truth we need all the equilibriums before we can hope to reach the pinnacle of success, because there are many who fell from grace after reaching the summit, famous people who lost their balance and fell into obscurity, or even took their own lives. There are many too who were rich, but lacked happiness, and also took their lives.

The list of priorities and sacrifices

If we go shopping and forget an essential item for the house or our children, we have to return to the shops again. We then learn to keep a list to help us remember everything we need. Our mind works by listing priorities. We may not envision this list in our minds, but it is there. If we neglect our children in favor of working, we do so because they are low down on our list of priorities. If we leave an appointment to deal with an emergency, we do so because at that moment the emergency is more important. If we lie to excuse ourselves, we are valuing our own benefit above the truth. Knowingly or not, we each create this list of priorities, which then governs our lives and actions.

Decisions are nothing but trade-offs between priorities, sacrificing those at the bottom. If we sacrifice the truth in favor of convenience, we should realize that we are harming our social equilibrium by risking being labeled a liar; and we are harming our spiritual equilibrium, because God knows our deeds and has forbidden lying.

Sacrifice has many aspects. A person who sacrifices convenience by telling the truth and suffering damaged relationships as a result, nevertheless gains equilibrium in return. Likewise, a person who sacrifices money to make others happy, or a person who sacrifices their relationships for a good cause, are taking their first steps to restoring their equilibriums.

Self-awareness is the first step towards correcting a wrong state. Most of our decisions are ultimately influenced by more than one equilibrium. Our spiritual equilibrium in particular has a part to play in most dimensions of our life, as reflecting on our spiritual equilibrium before taking a decision compels us to abide by what pleases God.

It is difficult to stay committed to our business when others are running away, or to be truthful when others are lying, and we may not get to see our children much because of our diligence at work. Fulfilling our duties at work is a minor test compared with running our lives year after year. But facing up to life's challenges shows that we are honest, and that we have faith, and that we trust in our faith and make it our top priority.

Questions and answers:

Q: I'm a very long way from spiritual equilibrium. What's the solution?

A: Re-read the obstacles to spiritual equilibrium. If that still doesn't help you, try to learn how to turn your intentions into actions, make a genuine resolution to get to know your Creator, and remind yourself every day that He will lead you.

Q: I'm a long way from social balance because I lack many of the skills needed. What should I do?

A: Make friends with sociable people and learn from them, as they represent the distilled knowledge of thousands of books. Ask yourself what puts you off from interacting with people, make a conscious effort to do it, and then evaluate your experience.

Q: I can't stop thinking about money. Money to me is paradise. How can I change my thoughts?

A: Spend a little time each day focusing on the disadvantages that come from having to earn money, as loose your precious time, This will give your brain a more balanced view of money, and your desires and behavior will then adjust themselves naturally.

Q: I'm very happy, and my happiness is constant and permanent. How can you say everlasting happiness doesn't exist, when I enjoy it?

A: Either tell us your secret, to benefit the rest of humanity; or tell us what you are taking to achieve it.

Q: I do whatever makes me happy without worrying about the equilibriums, and I see no reason to give up the pleasures I enjoy. Why should I change?

A: Have you watched the film about people in Florida who were warned about a hurricane, and sat there celebrating while waiting for it to arrive? Watch the film and see the hurricane uprooting them. Then ask yourself, what's your plan for your first night after death?

Q: Equilibriums are complicated and life is easy. Why complicate it?

A: Which life is easy? Do you mean the easy life that consists of going to work and coming home again? Or the very difficult life which involves doctors, wars, disease and earthquakes? Life is not easy, and nor is reaching contentment.

Bibliography

Brian Wansink, 2006. *Mindless Eating: Why We Eat More Than We Think*. Bantam Dell, United States.

Carol Dweck, 2006. *Mindset: The New Psychology of Success*. Ballantine Books, United States.

Dale Carnegie, mm, 1936. *How to Win Friends and Influence People. 1st ed.* Simon and Schuster, United States.

Daniel J. Siegel, 2010. *Mindsight: The New Science of Personal Transformation*. Bantam Books,United States.

Daniel J. Siegel, 2010. *The Mindful Therapist: A Clinician's Guide to Mindsight and Neural Integration*. W.W. Norton.

David Brooks, 2011. *The Social Animal: The Hidden Sources of Love, Character, and Achievement*. Random House.

Shawn Achor, 2010. *The Happiness Advantage: The Seven Principles of Positive Psychology That Fuel Success and Performance at Work*. Crown Business, United States.

Tal Ben-Shahar, 2008. *Happier: Learn the Secrets to Daily Joy and Lasting Fulfillment*. Tata McGraw-Hill Education, United States.

Journals

Angela Epstein, 2009. *Believe it or not, your lungs are six weeks old - and your taste buds just ten days! So how old is the rest of your*

body? [Online]. Availableat:http://www.dailymail.co.uk/health/
article-1219995/Believe-lungs-weeks-old--taste-buds-just-days-So-
old-rest-body.html [Accessed 29 March 2015].

Barry J. Zimmerman, 2002. *Theory into Practice. Becoming a Self-
Regulated Learner: An Overview*, 41.

Brian Wansink, Jeffery Sobal, Cornell University, 2007. *Environment
and Behavior. Mindless Eating:The 200 Daily Food Decisions We
Overlook*, 39, 106-123.

D. Buchanan Smith & 0. J. Robison, 1931. Animal Breeding Research
Department, University of Edinburgh. *The Average Ages of Cows
and Bulls in Six Breeds of Cattle,* 21, 136-149.

David Brown, 2010. *Ancient DNA shows interbreeding between Homo
sapiens and Neanderthal,* [Online]. Availableat: http://
www.washingtonpost.com/wpdyn/content/article/2010/05/06/
AR2010050604423.html [Accessed 29 May 2015].

Forbes Entrepreneurs. 90% Of Startups Fail. [ONLINE] Available at:
http://www.forbes.com/sites/neilpatel/2015/01/16/90-of-startups-
will-fail-heres-what-you-need-to-know-about-the-10/
#57b5a91e55e1 [Accessed 30 May 2015].

George Loewenstein, Tamar Krishnamurti, Jessica Kopsic, Daniel
McDonald, Carnegie Mellon University, 2015. Journal of Economic
Behavior & Organization. *Does Increased Sexual Frequency
Enhance Happiness*, 116, 206-218.

Gretchen Reynolds, 2015. *The Joy of (Just the Right Amount of) Sex*
[Online]. Available at: http://mobile.nytimes.com/blogs/well/

2015/06/25/the-joy-of-just-the-right-amount-of-sex[Accessed 29 May 2015].

J Happiness Stud (2012) 13:187–201

Julianne Holt-Lunstad and Timothy B. Smith. 2012. *Social relationships and mortality.* Social and Personality Psychology Compass, 6, 41– 53.WEBSITES:Mind Tools. Questioning Techniques. [ONLINE] Available at: https://www.mindtools.com/pages/article/ newTMC_88.htm. [Accessed 29 May 15].

Mark Levine, Steven V. Rumsey and Others, *Criteria and Recommendations for Vitamin C Intake*, JAMA, April 21, 1999 — Vol 281, No. 15 1415

Morten L. Kringelbach and Kent C. Berridge, 2012. *The Joyful Mind.* Proceedings of the International Multi conference on Computer Science and Information Technology pp Lifelong reinforcement and self-learning.

Nilly Mor, University of Illinois at Chicago, Jennifer Winquist, Valparaiso University, zz, 2015. *Self-Focused Attention and Negative Affect: A Meta-Analysis,* 128, 638-662.

Philip Brickman & Dan Coates, 1978. Journal of Personality and Social Psychology. *Lottery Winners and Accident Victims: Is Happiness Relative*, 36, 917-927.

Skills You Need. 1800. Types of Question. [ONLINE] Available at:http:// www.skillsyouneed.com/ips/question-types.html[Accessed 29 April 15].

Statistics New Zealand (2013). *Loneliness in New Zealand: Findings from the 2010 NZ General Social Survey*. Available from www.stats.govt.nz.

Wikipedia. 1800. Epistemology. [ONLINE] Available at:https://en.wikipedia.org/wiki/Epistemology.Accessed 29 March 15].

Yahoo Answers. 1800. *Difference between emotion and logic?* [ONLINE] Available at:https://answers.yahoo.com/question/index?qid=20100903120357AA3jXZQ. [Accessed 29 March 15].

Yahoo Answers. *How big is the universe in miles?* [ONLINE] Available at:https://answers.yahoo.com/question/index?qid=20090914170842AAnjS55. [Accessed 29 April 2015].

www.ingramcontent.com/pod-product-compliance
Lightning Source LLC
Chambersburg PA
CBHW060249290526

45789CB00001B/256